GLORY, GRIEF, *and the* GAVEL

GLORY, GRIEF, *and the* GAVEL

AN INSIDE GUIDE TO RUNNING FOR SPEAKER OF THE HOUSE

JOHN LEGANSKI

Since 1947
REGNERY
An Imprint of Skyhorse Publishing, Inc.

To my family, whose love and support made this journey possible.

PREFACE

To be elected president of the United States, you need approximately 80 million Americans to cast their ballot for you. Likewise to be elected vice president. However, to be elected Speaker of the House of Representatives—the third-highest-ranking official in the country, second in line to the presidency—you need only 218 votes, fewer than is required to win most local school board races.

The voters in the contest for Speaker are the 435 members of the House of Representatives, a group of individuals as eclectic and energetic as the constituents they represent—a true mosaic of America. Some members have been in office for forty years. Others have been in Washington for less than four days. But each member's vote counts the same, and each vote is accompanied by its own unique—sometimes deeply personal—history.

Over the years, the role of Speaker has changed. Some of the earliest Speakers were chosen simply for their ability to loudly project their voices and maintain order over the rambunctious chamber. Others had national prominence and name recognition before their election as Speaker—like Henry Clay of Kentucky, a former senator so highly regarded by his peers that he was elected to the top job on the very first day of his freshman term in the House. Speaker James K. Polk, meanwhile, went on to serve as the 11th President of the United States.

You might be familiar with the names of some of the other more noteworthy and influential individuals to wield the gavel, such as Joseph Cannon of Illinois, Sam Rayburn of Texas, Tip O'Neill of Massachusetts, and Newt Gingrich of Georgia—each of whom molded the position to their personality and are responsible for expanding the powers and responsibilities of the office into what they are today.

Through 2022, only fifty-four individuals in our nation's history had ascended to the speakership—fewer than would fill the first two rows of the House chamber if they were all seated next to one another. By comparison, America saw forty-six presidents occupy the White House over that same period of time. Yet while mountains of scholarship and literature exist around the presidency and the famous campaigns that produced our commanders in chief, relatively little has been written about the equally intense and enormously consequential campaigns that have been waged to elect the first officer listed in the Constitution, the Speaker.

That is, until now.

What follows is a first-person, inside account of the election for the 55th Speaker of the House—the most contentious, fascinating, and widely watched contest for the office that America has witnessed in well over a century.

Go behind the scenes into the backroom strategy sessions, unreported meetings, and secret hideaway conversations that occurred throughout the US Capitol in the days and weeks leading up to the 2023 floor fight—the proverbial "rooms where it happened."

Sit under the bright lights of the House floor, a place where you're never quite sure who is your friend and who is your foe at any given moment of the day—and where clashes among members almost, quite literally, come to blows.

Trace the decade of tumult in the Republican Party that precipitated this internecine struggle and understand its ramifications for the institution of the House and the nation at large moving forward.

And experience all of this through the eyes of a top congressional aide, someone who first fell in love with our nation's capital on an eighth grade field trip, rose from intern to one of the most influential staffers in the House of Representatives, and occupied a front-row seat to the epic tug-of-war that captivated viewers across the country and around the world over the course of five dramatic days in January 2023—the effects of which are still being felt to this day.

CAST OF CHARACTERS

Speaker of the House

Kevin McCarthy, Republican of California

Dan Meyer, Chief of Staff

James Min, Natalie Joyce, John Leganski, Matthew Sparks, Deputy Chiefs of Staff

Machalagh Carr, General Counsel

Members of House Leadership

Steve Scalise, Republican of Louisiana, Majority Leader

Tom Emmer, Republican of Minnesota, Majority Whip

Guy Reschenthaler, Republican of Pennsylvania, Chief Deputy Whip

Patrick McHenry, Republican of North Carolina, Chair, House Financial Services Committee

Garret Graves, Republican of Louisiana, Chair, Elected Leadership Committee

Jim Jordan, Republican of Ohio, Chair, House Judiciary Committee

Members of the House Freedom Caucus

Scott Perry, Republican of Pennsylvania, Chair, House Freedom Caucus (January 2022–December 2023)

Bob Good, Republican of Virginia, Chair, House Freedom Caucus (January 2024–September 2024)

Dan Bishop, Republican of North Carolina

Byron Donalds, Republican of Florida

Ralph Norman, Republican of South Carolina

Chip Roy, Republican of Texas

Tim Reitz, Executive Director

Matt Gaetz, Republican of Florida, Freedom Caucus ally

Former Members of the House

John Boehner, Republican of Ohio, Speaker of the House
(January 2011–October 2015)

Paul Ryan, Republican of Wisconsin, Speaker of the House
(October 2015–January 2019)

Eric Cantor, Republican of Virginia, Majority Leader
(January 2011–August 2014)

Mark Meadows, Republican of North Carolina, Chair, House Freedom
Caucus (January 2017–October 2019)

Uneasy lies the head that wears a crown.
—King Henry IV, Part II, *1596*
William Shakespeare

PART I

ORIGINS

———

CHAPTER 1

A BOY FROM BAKERSFIELD

It should have been the greatest day of my professional life. After more than a decade of setbacks and breakthroughs, we were on the cusp of electing my boss, Kevin McCarthy, to be the 55th Speaker of the US House of Representatives.

My phone buzzed nonstop with congratulatory texts and well-wishes from family, friends, and colleagues—past and present, near and far.

Supporters began to file into the building, our office filled with the smell of catered Five Guys burgers and fries. My wife, Giulia, even brought her parents and some of our closest friends to watch—all dressed for the occasion and ready to take their seats in the public gallery that overlooked the House floor.

Everyone was jubilant, smiling, giving each other high fives and hugs.

Unfortunately, I could not share in their joy. Instead, I sat alone in an empty office, feeling totally broken and helpless.

Unlike them, I knew the truth: We did not have the votes to win.

Abraham Lincoln is said to have remarked, "I have been driven many times upon my knees by the overwhelming conviction that I had nowhere else to go."

In that moment, I understood some small measure of what Lincoln meant.

But I am getting ahead of myself. We'll come back to this later.

* * *

I can still remember my first time riding up the Capitol South escalator and seeing the shining white marble of the Cannon House Office Building come into focus.

It was a warm spring day—April 2, 2012—and I proudly donned my least ill-fitting hand-me-down suit, allowing myself to briefly get lost in the wonder of what I was about to undertake.

In my hands, I carefully secured a piece of paper listing the office of a California congressman I had never met: *"326 Cannon House Office Building—Rep. Kevin McCarthy (R-CA)."*

Prior to that week, the only other time I had been to our nation's capital was on my eighth-grade class field trip. But even then, I felt a certain reverence and awe for both the history of the place and for the people who made our government run on a daily basis. When I began to contemplate where to pursue a career after college graduation, it was an easy choice to pick the city that I fell in love with all those years ago.

Stanford University's DC program boasted plenty of internship openings in the offices of prominent California Democrats—Speaker Nancy Pelosi and Senators Barbara Boxer and Dianne Feinstein, to name a few. I had to gently inform the program directors, however, that I was one of the "others" on our liberal-leaning campus—namely, a registered Republican.

My boss-to-be for the next ten weeks was a man named Kevin McCarthy, a fourth-term congressman who served as majority whip, the third ranking leadership position in the House of Representatives tasked with corralling and cajoling enough votes to pass any given piece of legislation.

McCarthy, or "Kevin" as he insisted we call him, was a homegrown talent, a risk-taker, and someone seemingly destined for something greater—an individual whom I quickly grew to learn from and admire. And little did I know, but my planned ten-week internship with his office would go on to become a ten-year career on Capitol Hill that increasingly centered around one mission: elect Kevin McCarthy as Speaker of the House.

* * *

The son of a firefighter's household, Kevin Owen McCarthy was born on January 26, 1965, the youngest of three children.

The McCarthy family grew up in Bakersfield, California, a hot and dusty blue-collar city in the Central Valley dotted with oil rigs, carrot fields, and almond orchards—and home to the late country music legends Merle Haggard and Buck Owens. To me, it always felt like a slice of Texas had been accidentally dropped in the middle of the Golden State.

Kevin attended Bakersfield High School, where he played football for the Drillers—their mascot a nod to the many oil wells on the horizon—and met his wife-to-be, Judy. The high school sweethearts would later raise their two children a few miles up the road in the first home they ever bought together.

At age twenty, Kevin won $5,000 during the inaugural week of the California State Lottery—odds 40,000 to 1—investing the bulk of his winnings in the stock market, while opening a small sandwich shop named "Kevin O's Deli." The proceeds from that business would eventually help pay for an undergraduate degree and an MBA from California State University, Bakersfield.

But from where I sat, Kevin's true passion was found in politics.

In 1987, he applied to be an intern in the office of Bakersfield's Congressman at the time, Bill Thomas. Somewhat astonishingly, however, Kevin's initial application was rejected. He would later cite this rejection as grounds for accepting some of the largest intern classes known to Capitol Hill, my spring 2012 class included.

A second application proved to be the charm, with Kevin eventually being promoted to work as Thomas's district director, an important position that put him where he was at his best: face-to-face with people, from constituents and business leaders to local officials and other concerned citizens.

Over the same period of time, Kevin was active with Young Republicans, chairing the California chapter in 1995 before chairing the Young Republican National Federation from 1999 to 2001, a role that afforded him the opportunity to speak before the Republican National Convention of 2000 that nominated then-Governor George W. Bush to take on then-Senator Al Gore for the presidency.

By all accounts, Kevin was a creative and energetic organizer. One memorable rendezvous saw him orchestrate a Freedom Train caravan with longtime friend and future GOP power broker Jeff Miller. The caravan departed from

Chicago and picked up Young Republicans from city to city en route to the Republican National Convention in San Diego—with reporters from MTV News' *Unfiltered* on board for the ride.

Kevin's experiences with Young Republicans also put him in touch with several individuals he would one day work alongside in the halls of Congress. This included an equally gregarious and ambitious young man from New Orleans, future House Majority Leader Steve Scalise, as well as a brash helicopter pilot from the Pennsylvania Air National Guard, future chair of the House Freedom Caucus Scott Perry. Keep those two names handy—Scalise and Perry—as we move forward.

In 2000, Kevin officially threw his hat into the political ring, winning election as a Kern Community College District trustee. Two years later, he ran for and was elected to the California State Assembly. His leadership skills were evident to his colleagues even as a freshman, and he was chosen to serve as Republican floor leader—the top leadership position in the minority—in his very first term.

In Sacramento, Kevin began to cultivate the skills and style that would define his approach to leadership. He rented a house not far from the state capitol where he and his fellow Republicans would live, socialize, and strategize.

"People would work during the day in the legislature and we would have events at night, but only for members," Kevin recalled. Those events ranged from card games and playing pool to hosting bipartisan barbecues. "It was a place where members could go and talk about what happened during the day, and we would get a lot of work done there."

Kevin's fellow California assembly members and senators at the time included Republicans Jeff Denham, Tom McClintock, and Doug LaMalfa, as well as Democrat and future mayor of Los Angeles Karen Bass—all of whom would later go on to serve together in the US House.

* * *

About a year into Kevin's first term in the Assembly, California residents delivered a political earthquake—voting for the first time in state history to recall an incumbent governor. As if the result was not already dramatic enough, the referendum saw embattled Democratic Governor Gray Davis replaced by none other than Republican political newcomer and movie megastar Arnold Schwarzenegger.

While Sacramento turned into a media circus seemingly overnight, Kevin and the new governor quickly developed a rapport, working closely together to notch victories in the face of a Democrat-led Assembly and Senate on issues ranging from reforms to the state budget to repealing an unpopular vehicle registration fee increase dubbed "the car tax" by candidate Schwarzenegger.

But my favorite anecdote that Kevin shared from his years of working with Governor Schwarzenegger was the former movie star's preferred respite after a tough day in the political arena, a phone call that began and ended in that unmistakable accent with a simple request: *"Kevin . . . Let's go shopping."*

In a matter of minutes, the governor's SUVs would arrive and whisk the group away to a nearby mall where they would engage in a little retail therapy. On the scale of vices that I have personally witnessed among legislators and staffers in Washington, there were certainly worse ways to deal with the daily stresses of the job.

Importantly for our story, Kevin's time with the celebrity-turned-politician in Sacramento gave him unique insights that would come in handy down the road, specifically, as they applied to one Donald J. Trump. Kevin was not only able to spot the rise of Trump in 2016 far before many others in the Beltway chattering class could but also gained valuable experience in translating the mechanics of governing to someone who was not otherwise steeped in the legislative process.

"I think there were a lot of similarities: They were both known to the country before they ran, they were both very intuitive and prided themselves on being good negotiators, and they both followed what I would consider meek men in build and character—Gray Davis and [Barack] Obama," Kevin noted. "When you think about Trump and the size of his rallies, Arnold had those. And these were people who were not normally engaged but were getting engaged in politics because they believed in those individuals."

Though decades apart, Kevin added that both Schwarzenegger's and Trump's rallies shared a common theme song in the playlist, as well: "We're

Not Gonna Take It" by Twisted Sister—emblematic of the defiant ethos that animated their respective campaigns.

Even so, as much fun as working alongside the most recognizable governor in the country was, Kevin had greater ambitions than being in the permanent legislative minority in Sacramento. So when Bakersfield Congressman Bill Thomas announced in March 2006 that he would retire at the end of the term, Kevin did not hesitate to jump at the opportunity, earning the endorsement of his former boss and winning the general election for the safely Republican Central Valley seat with over 70 percent of the vote.

With that, just four years after first being elected to local office, the boy from Bakersfield was off to Washington, DC.

CHAPTER 2

YOUNG GUNS

While the 2006 election was a personally joyous one in the McCarthy household, it was a disastrous cycle nationwide for Republicans. Fatigue with President George W. Bush and the wars in Iraq and Afghanistan, as well as a high-profile lobbying and bribery scandal that embroiled Hill Republicans known as the Jack Abramoff affair, contributed to Democrats flipping control of both the House and Senate.

Democrats cheered as countless rising stars won election to the House, including future senators Peter Welch of Vermont, Chris Murphy of Connecticut, Kirsten Gillibrand of New York, Mazie Hirono of Hawaii, and Joe Donnelly of Indiana, as well as future governor and 2024 vice presidential nominee Tim Walz of Minnesota.

A change in the House majority also meant the election of a new Speaker—the first woman as well as the first Californian to ever wield the gavel, Nancy Pelosi.

Meanwhile, Kevin was one of only thirteen Republican freshman representatives to be elected, one of the smallest classes in recent memory. Classmates of his included such individuals as Tea Party darling Michele Bachmann of Minnesota and wrestling champion and future founding member of the House Freedom Caucus, Jim Jordan of Ohio.

No pomp and circumstance awaited these new Republican representatives. Instead, they were merely treated to the realities of life shifting into the House minority and all the "perks" that came with it, like the last choice in committee assignments and office space.

Internally, Kevin was chosen by his fellow freshmen to be their class representative on the powerful and secretive Steering Committee, a panel responsible for doling out committee assignments and selecting individuals to chair the various House committees. For reference, this same slot was once held by a young freshman from Georgia by the name of Newt Gingrich when he was first elected to the House in 1978.

Serving on the Steering Committee allowed Kevin to better understand the inner workings of Congress from day one and gain perhaps the most valuable insight any leader could ask for—an intimate understanding of what every other member aspired to and hoped for in their own career trajectory. Such information was worth its weight in gold for anyone looking to ascend the leadership hierarchy, and being one of the few individuals allowed to staff the Steering Committee was one of my personal favorite responsibilities during my time on the Hill.

On top of that, the role put Kevin in the same room with the regional power brokers of the Republican conference—individuals from whom he would learn the ropes and look to for counsel over the years—as well as existing committee chairs and members of leadership, like House Minority Leader and Speaker-in-waiting, John Boehner of Ohio.

* * *

In advance of the 2008 presidential election, Minority Leader Boehner tapped Kevin to chair the committee responsible for drafting the official Republican Party platform. Kevin initially asked if he did something wrong to receive such an assignment, which is typically a fraught exercise of careful wordsmithing between competing ideological factions. But he dutifully took on the task nonetheless, working with state party chairs and activists to hammer out an agreement on the campaign framework that would attempt to unify the GOP heading into the general election.

Although Republicans fared poorly at the polls in 2008 with the historic election of President Barack Obama leading to an additional twenty-one seat pickup for Democrats in the House, Kevin was singled out for another promotion, this time as the top lieutenant—or "chief deputy whip"—for newly elevated Minority Whip Eric Cantor of Virginia.

This assignment was one of the most demanding in the House, allowing Kevin to further interact with fellow members of the Republican conference and more deeply understand their individual priorities. Over the years, he would deploy this knowledge masterfully, developing a near-encyclopedic grasp of the demographic makeup and political dynamics of each member's district, oftentimes knowing their seat better than they knew it themselves.

Ditto for their personal backgrounds. It was not an uncommon occurrence for a member's child to be wished a happy birthday or their spouse to be congratulated on an anniversary by Kevin before that member had even gotten out of bed in the morning.

In addition, the role helped Kevin cut his teeth in the all-important art of whipping, rallying the conference to unite against what the leadership team viewed as the woefully out-of-touch and overreaching agenda of President Obama. Together with Boehner and the rest of the leadership team, Cantor and Kevin successfully whipped all House Republicans to vote no on both of Obama's signature measures: the economic stimulus bill and the Affordable Care Act or "Obamacare." These two legislative showdowns completely dominated the national political conversation at the start of President Obama's first term and set the stage for the upcoming midterm elections of 2010.

* * *

While all of the above experiences were formative, everyone knew that the number one job of the minority was to become the majority. And it was in this arena where Kevin truly excelled, raising massive sums of money, recruiting new and captivating candidates to run for Congress, and generally scheming up creative ways to elect more Republicans to the House.

It was certainly not an easy task at that time. Republicans found themselves at only 178 members in 2009, a deep minority fully forty seats away from the requisite 218 for a majority. Likewise, President Obama enjoyed approval ratings into the mid 60s throughout much of his first year in office and pundits openly mocked the notion that a House majority flip was in the offing as his first term hummed along.

Still, Kevin made a compelling case, oftentimes traveling to potential recruits' homes in far-flung corners of the country and sitting down at their kitchen tables to make a personal appeal. He even devised his own formula for what was required to win back the House backed by historical data points and trends, from the congressional generic ballot to individual member disbursements.

Part of the equation was retirements. After all, it was much easier to defeat a first-time candidate than a longtime incumbent. In particular, Kevin identified Democrats who were more senior, had smaller campaign war chests, or had faced closer-than-expected results in the most recent election. He surmised that this group of members had less fire in the belly and were perhaps more open to gracefully exiting if a credible challenger emerged. For good measure, he would flood these Democrats' offices with robocalls and buy negative billboard advertisements along the route between their homes and the closest airport—all to make them question each and every day whether running again was really what they wanted.

"If your mother calls and tells you an ad is too negative against your opponent," he would advise candidates, "then double the buy."

In total, seventeen House Democrats ultimately chose retirement rather than standing for reelection in 2010, creating valuable open seat pickup opportunities.

On the other end of the spectrum, Kevin worked to rattle greener members, the freshmen and sophomores who were still becoming known in their districts and could be better defined by Republican campaign attacks. The effort proved successful as a whopping thirty-four Democratic freshmen and sophomores would go on to be defeated in 2010.

Kevin's studies into past instances of House majority flips also revealed other patterns. He noticed that around the fifth term in office, many members would begin to spend less money on communicating with their constituents back home—usually in conjunction with them receiving a plum committee assignment in Washington. This left the incumbents uniquely vulnerable to a challenge, even if they had prevailed in the prior election by a wide margin.

Military veterans made for effective messengers to initiate such electoral challenges, which led Kevin to enlist the likes of Chris Gibson of New

York, Steve Stivers of Ohio, Rick Crawford of Arkansas, and Allen West of Florida.

The same could be said for medical doctors during that period in time when health-care reform was roiling both Republican voters and independents alike, yielding recruits such as Dr. Andy Harris of Maryland and Dr. Larry Bucshon of Indiana.

Plus-size auctioneer Billy Long said yes in Missouri, as did Tennessee cotton farmer Stephen Fincher. Other noteworthy first-time candidates included future Senator Tim Scott of South Carolina, as well as future Governor of South Dakota and Secretary of Homeland Security Kristi Noem.

Bonus points were given to candidates who demonstrated an ability to fundraise, whether they had served in elected office before or not.

"If you can't ask everyone on your Christmas card list for money," Kevin would warn, "then you probably shouldn't run for Congress."

Finally, Kevin found that most every recent House majority flip included at least one former professional athlete in the class. To be safe, he recruited three to run in the primaries, with former Philadelphia Eagles offensive lineman Jon Runyan keeping the streak alive after successfully capturing a congressional seat along the Jersey Shore.

"I'd call Runyan and say: 'If you win, we win the majority,'—just because that was a data point," Kevin joked.

* * *

At the national level, the Republican Party needed a rebrand, as well. The "culture of corruption" label deployed by Democrats in 2006 to great effect seemed to stick. If Republicans were to take back the House, they would need something fresh and exciting to signal a clean break from the past.

Enter the "Young Guns," a nickname coined by Fred Barnes of *The Weekly Standard* in a splashy piece that profiled a trio of new age conservative leaders.

Eric Cantor—the serious, measured Virginian—was dubbed the group's leader.

"I'm convinced," Barnes wrote, "Eric Cantor will be Speaker or majority leader the next time Republicans control the House."

Paul Ryan—the wonky Wisconsinite and future vice presidential nominee—would be the thinker, tasked with balancing the budget and finding a solution to ensure the longtime solvency of America's entitlement programs, either as chair of the Budget or Ways and Means Committee.

Lastly, Kevin McCarthy—the sunny Californian—would be the strategist, focused on helping Republicans win more elections, more often.

"As for McCarthy, he'll be right behind Cantor in the leadership, either as majority leader or whip," Barnes wrote.

"And someday, if Cantor steps aside, even House Speaker."

* * *

Drawing upon his experience leading the 2008 platform committee, Kevin worked to craft a new campaign agenda for the midterms called the Pledge to America—part homage and part imitation of former Speaker Newt Gingrich's famous Contract with America that was credited with propelling Republicans to a historic victory in the 1994 midterms that ended forty years in the minority.

By the time November 2010 rolled around, these efforts combined with an ascendant and energetic Tea Party movement managed to produce a red wave that touched down from sea to shining sea. Republicans netted a total of 63 new seats in the House, the biggest win for any party in a House midterm election since 1938 and more than enough for control of the chamber. A few blocks up Pennsylvania Avenue, President Obama called the results "a shellacking."

Dozens of these new House Republican freshmen were individuals who had been handpicked and convinced to run by Kevin, most having never before served in elected office. And thanks to the flip in control, each of the top leaders in the chamber received a promotion: McCarthy to majority whip, the number three job; Cantor to majority leader, second-in-command; and John Boehner to Speaker of the House.

The gavel was officially passed from outgoing Speaker Pelosi to incoming Speaker Boehner on January 3, 2011.

"The American people have humbled us," Boehner stated in his opening remarks to the chamber. "They have refreshed our memories as to just how temporary the privilege to serve is. They have reminded us that everything here is on loan from them. That includes this gavel, which I accept cheerfully and gratefully, knowing I am but its caretaker."

In a sign of confidence and overall Republican jubilation, Boehner received the vote of all 246 of his Republican colleagues on the House floor—with each member-elect rising one by one, alphabetically, to announce their selection.

Little did we know that would be the last time a Speaker nominee would be elected with the unanimous support of their party on the floor for more than a decade.

CHAPTER 3

CURSE OF THE MAJORITY LEADER

Tuesday, June 10, 2014

"Eric is losing his primary . . . badly."

The words hit me like a ton of bricks.

Eric, of course, referred to then-Majority Leader Eric Cantor, the powerful Virginian lawmaker who was presumed to be a future Speaker of the House. Yet here he was at risk of losing his seat in Congress entirely to a small-town economics professor named *Dave Brat*?

I hadn't even realized there was a primary in Virginia that day. Apparently, I wasn't the only one.

* * *

At that time, I had been working on the Hill for just under a year since graduation. I was first hired as a staff assistant in Kevin's majority whip office, an entry-level position answering phones, compiling news clips, and giving Capitol tours to constituents with a starting salary of $30,000 per year. I have to imagine my parents were at least a little bit concerned that this was what four years of a Stanford education had produced—but if so, they did their best to hide it and be supportive.

In an effort to save money, my best friend from growing up, Joe Gierut, and I rented a small apartment off the Van Ness metro stop that we affectionately dubbed "the Compound" given its concrete resemblance to a prison complex. To complete the look, we furnished our place with a used kitchen table and chairs set we bought for $75 on Craigslist.

After a few months, however, I received a promotion to the part of the office that I had found myself most drawn to since my days as an intern: the "floor team," the central nervous system of the whip's vote-counting operation.

Between the Speaker, majority leader, and majority whip, fewer than a dozen staffers worked on the floor team any given year, with each leadership office having its own unique roles and responsibilities that helped the institution of the House of Representatives function on a day-to-day basis.

In the whip's office, our primary job was to help Kevin canvass all members of the party, determine how they planned to vote on critical upcoming pieces of legislation, and "whip" enough votes for a measure to pass.

In practice, whipping involved quickly fanning out and distributing printed cards to the fifty or so members of our deputy whip team during a vote series. This card detailed the top-line bullet points of the measure we were hoping to pass, the member assignments that each deputy whip was responsible for, and their corresponding responses ranging from "yes," "lean yes," and "undecided," to "lean no," and the dreaded "no." Our team would input these responses into what we called the "whip check" and then devise a plan with Kevin and the leadership team for how to best move 218 members into the yes column.

In between working to pass high-level measures like annual government funding bills and other legislative priorities, those of us on the floor staff were also on hand to help members with whatever they might need to do their job—be it offering an amendment at the right time, making a parliamentary inquiry, or fielding questions on everything from the current bill under debate to their most frequently asked question: "When are last votes?"

"Be confident, concise, and correct," our floor director, John Stipicevic, told me my first week when it came to answering members' questions—sound advice that I did my best to heed while keeping pace with the fast-moving and rambunctious floor.

Of course, members were just people, too, and I gradually learned their unique quirks. Some wanted to talk about last night's game. Others had a one-liner or dad joke ready for every encounter—and appreciated one in return. A few had strong opinions about what types of gum we kept at the leadership desk—so we took care to stock up on their favorites. After all, a happy member is more likely to vote "yes."

In that regard, the job was more a study in psychology than anything. Over time, many of the carrots and sticks that were famously used to build support for legislative measures in yesteryear had either been done away with or rendered moot. Think, for example, district-specific earmarks or rewarding allies with plum committee assignments.

Instead, the modern art of whipping in the House of Representatives was built on persuasion—either via charm or via implied consequence—and Kevin was a pro at knowing exactly what buttons to push with what members at what time.

Over the course of one particularly contentious vote, I saw him flip a member from the South by putting his arm around them, cracking a few jokes, and happily cajoling them into voting yes—only to minutes later storm over to a member from the Northeast, bark in their face, and storm off angrily, just in time for them to put their card in the voting box and switch from no to yes. Understanding how and when to deploy this type of good-cop, bad-cop approach was simply not something you could learn in school, and it was a privilege to witness up close.

To prepare for my new job, I was instructed to make and memorize flash cards with the names and faces of all 247 House Republicans—a surprisingly tricky task when the majority of our members then were older, white men who largely looked the same.

One member who needed no flash card, however, was Majority Leader Eric Cantor.

A frequent foil to President Obama, Cantor was one of the most important power players in Washington at that time—not to mention one of Kevin's closest friends. An experienced legislator and sharp tactician, he maintained a hot-and-cold rivalry with Speaker Boehner as the presumed heir apparent to his job. Over the years, I would learn that such tension was par for the course when it came to the number one and number two officeholders atop any congressional leadership hierarchy.

None of those future plans would matter, though, if Cantor did not retain his seat in the House.

* * *

Back in the office, we kept hitting refresh on the Virginia Secretary of State's website only to continue reaching the same conclusion: Cantor was going to lose—the first sitting House majority leader to lose a primary since the position was created in 1899.

Immediately, my heart turned to the friends and colleagues I had grown close with in his office, several of whom had served as mentors to me along the way, including Tim Pataki, Sarah Kish Morgan, and Chris Vieson, as well as my future business partners, Kyle Nevins and Steve Stombres.

As anyone who has worked on the Hill can attest, you spend a lot of time with one another, and your colleagues become almost like a second family. I can't imagine the thought had crossed any of their minds that something like this was possible. One day, you are the toast of the town—the next, you are looking for a new job.

Indeed, I would come to understand that all House Republican leadership jobs should come with a warning label: CAUTION: THIS WILL END IN TEARS.

Shortly after 10 p.m. eastern time, Cantor took the stage in Richmond alongside his wife to address a group of shell-shocked supporters gathered at what was presumed to be a victory party. A hundred miles up the road in DC, our team huddled around the conference room television to watch, still in disbelief.

"Obviously, we came up short," he began.

I excused myself after a few minutes to get some fresh air, only to find that one of our more tenured staffers had just puked in a trash can beside their desk. At least I wasn't alone in my nervousness about what might happen next.

* * *

For much of the twentieth century, the second-ranking slot in the House of Representatives was a natural springboard to the speakership. Majority leaders were elevated to Speaker on a fairly regular basis, from Republican Nicholas Longworth of Ohio to a string of Democrats including Sam Rayburn of Texas, John W. McCormack of Massachusetts, Carl Albert of Oklahoma, Tip O'Neill of Massachusetts, Jim Wright of Texas, and Tom Foley of Washington.

Toward the turn of the century, however, the majority leader position was not a springboard to the speakership so much as a curse to those who sought the top job: the Curse of the Majority Leader, if you will. And this particular hex proved to be especially acute on the Republican side of the aisle. To wit:

HALE BOGGS (D-LA), 1972

While serving as majority leader, Hale Boggs embarked on a campaign trip for Representative Nick Begich of Alaska. Tragically, on October 16, 1972, their twin-engine aircraft went missing in inclement winter weather on a flight between Anchorage and Juneau. A lengthy search and rescue operation ensued, but was suspended after thirty-nine days. No trace of the plane nor the four men traveling on board was ever found. The tragedy was also the subject of a podcast called *Missing in Alaska* that raised questions about alleged involvement by members of the Mafia in the plane's disappearance.

DICK ARMEY (R-TX), 1999

Dick Armey served as second-in-command under Speaker Newt Gingrich following the Republican Revolution of 1994. When Gingrich stepped away from leadership after a disappointing midterm election amid the impeachment of President Bill Clinton, Armey found that his standing had been diminished, as well, needing multiple ballots to beat back a challenge for his post in the 1998 internal conference elections. By the time Republican Speaker-designee Bob Livingston of Louisiana shocked his colleagues in announcing his own resignation from Congress as a result of marital infidelities, Armey was too weakened to mount a serious challenge for Speaker. Instead, the gavel fell to "Accidental Speaker" Dennis Hastert of Illinois—who later pled guilty to paying hush money to conceal sexual abuses he committed against his students as a high school teacher.

DICK GEPHARDT (D-MO), 2003

Following a briefly promising yet ultimately failed presidential primary bid in 1998, Dick Gephardt was elected majority leader by House Democrats to serve behind then-Speaker Tom Foley. When Gingrich faced a potential coup among House Republicans in 1997, there was a brief window in which Gephardt could have been elected Speaker if he had convinced a small handful of moderate Republicans who were upset with Gingrich to cross party lines and support his candidacy. Such a vote never materialized, however, and he departed Congress before Democrats next seized majority control in 2006.

TOM DeLAY (R-TX), 2005

After serving as whip for eight years, Tom DeLay—or "The Hammer" as he came to be known for his aggressive arm-twisting tactics—was elected majority leader in 2003 following Armey's retirement from Congress. In 2005, DeLay became the first congressional leader in history to be indicted, as prosecutors charged him with multiple counts of money laundering and conspiracy related to illegal campaign finance activities during the 2002 Texas state elections. He was forced to resign his position as leader and make a pledge to not seek the position in the future, later being implicated in the Jack Abramoff lobbying scandal.

ROY BLUNT (R-MO), 2006

In the wake of DeLay stepping down, Republicans turned to Roy Blunt to serve as majority leader on an acting basis. Several months later, with DeLay's announcement that he would not seek to regain his former position, Blunt quickly declared that he would run to permanently serve as majority leader. While Blunt was the presumed favorite and even issued a press release stating he had secured a majority of commitments inside the conference for the role, he lost the race in an upset to then-Chair of the Education and the Workforce Committee John Boehner, who secured enough commitments on a deciding second ballot to edge out Blunt by a total of 122 to 109.

STENY HOYER (D-MD), 2022

Steny Hoyer's chief impediment to the speakership was introduced to him in 1963 in the form of a fellow junior staffer by the name of Nancy Pelosi. Over the course of the next six decades, the two would be intertwined in an on-again, off-again power struggle—one that came to a head in a decisive 2001 race for minority whip that saw Pelosi prevail over Hoyer by a vote of 118–95. Hoyer served two separate stints as majority leader, never to reach the gavel.

* * *

As for Eric Cantor, he announced that he would step down from the majority leader position and retire from Congress entirely at the start of the upcoming August recess. His departure brought the tally to the six most recent majority leaders failing to reach the Speaker's chair following at least one full term as leader. Put differently, the last time a majority leader was elevated to Speaker following a full term in the office was in 1989—before I was even born.

None of this should be taken as a knock on any of these individuals. By all accounts, they were incredibly skillful and adept politicians in their own right. After all, they did end up being elected to one of the most powerful positions in Washington, charged with deciding what bills would come to the floor and overseeing the work of all House committees.

Rather, the true curse is that this second-in-line post simply leaves you in purgatory for too long. Always the bridesmaid, never the bride.

Unlike the presidency, which is contested every four years, the position of Speaker could come available at any time or never at all if your party was confined to the minority for long enough. If and when the stars would happen to align for a majority leader, there was a good chance you had already earned too many enemies or too much scar tissue to put together a winning coalition. As the saying goes, "Friends come and go, but enemies accumulate."

Rightly or wrongly, you were held responsible for the decisions made by past Speakers, even though your job at the end of the day was to execute the play call made by that Speaker.

"Everyone who becomes a chairman thinks they did it all by themselves," Kevin would joke. "Everyone who loses blames me."

Finally, depending on the size of any given majority, it would only take a few disgruntled members to block a Speaker's bid on the House floor—a once-rare tactic that would come more into vogue in the years to follow.

At the staff level, I am fairly confident that we were not fully aware of the extent of this curse at the time. Even if we were, I don't think it would have stopped what happened next.

"I don't know who it is that will actually be running," Cantor told the assembled media the next day when asked who he supported for his position in leadership. "I can tell you that if my dear friend and colleague Kevin McCarthy does decide to run, I think he'd make an outstanding majority leader, and I will be backing him with my full support."

And so, with Cantor's endorsement and the encouragement of his fellow House Republicans, Kevin launched his run for the position of majority leader on June 11, 2014. Our vote-counting operation went into high gear on a dime, swiftly locking up support from all corners of the conference and depriving any would-be challengers of oxygen.

A last-minute bid by Raul Labrador of Idaho—who famously did not even have most of his colleagues' cell phone numbers handy when he launched his run—was easily dispatched with. Free advice if you're running for leadership: Asking another member for their support should not be the first time they ever receive a phone call from you.

Even so, Labrador represented a small yet growing conservative faction in our conference that only grew more emboldened in the years following Cantor's defeat and whom we would become intimately aware of—a group you know as the House Freedom Caucus or HFC.

The events of that June week were also foundational for me as a twenty-three-year-old staffer who had only known good times in Washington. The night of Cantor's defeat, I wrote down two important lessons in my journal that I would internalize moving forward: "Expect the unexpected" and "Don't take anything for granted—especially in this line of work."

* * *

Down the leadership line, Kevin's ascent to leader triggered an opening for the number three position of majority whip that was won by Louisiana's Steve Scalise, Kevin's aforementioned Young Republicans friend from chapter 1. Scalise centered his campaign on the message of putting someone from a reliably red state at the leadership table—a message that some suggested we back in the hopes of appeasing the newly restive right flank that was clamoring for more conservative voices at the top.

"We're evolving our leadership in a conservative direction," said fellow Louisianan John Fleming after Scalise's victory in the whip race. Fleming added a prediction that Kevin was "good for another two years" before he would also be replaced by a more conservative colleague.

None of that noise mattered to us at the time. Instead, it seemed as though fate had put the forty-nine-year-old Kevin McCarthy on a fast track in the House, along with those of us who had started on the ground floor of his now quickly expanding team.

Almost overnight, he and our staff would have to learn an entirely new set of roles and responsibilities that fell under the majority leader's purview—from establishing what days the House would be in session and choosing what bills would come to the floor to managing the committee chairs and overseeing the broader legislative agenda. Whatever misfortunes or calamities had befallen those majority leaders before us, we were determined to not let the same happen to our guy.

"I'll make one promise: I will work every single day to make sure this conference has the courage to lead with the wisdom to listen," Kevin told the press in his trademark sunny tone after winning the post. "And we'll turn this country around."

Unfortunately, curses are an awfully stubborn thing to break.

CHAPTER 4

THE POWER OF THE HOLY SPIRIT

"Boehner is resigning."

"Holy shit. Are you sure?" I asked.

My colleague, Ben Howard, assured me that he was, having directly run up from that morning's Republican conference meeting, which was originally scheduled to discuss the upcoming September 30 government funding deadline until it took a dramatic turn.

Kevin was made aware only minutes before the news was made public, with Boehner pulling him outside the room before the meeting began to say: "You gotta get ready. I'm gonna step down."

"I didn't see it coming," Kevin later remarked.

Just over a year since the Cantor loss, it felt like "déjà vu all over again" as Yogi Berra would say—another whiplash-inducing turn of events.

* * *

For Boehner, the retirement announcement was almost certainly a welcome respite from the constant coup chatter that surrounded his speakership, then a year into its third term.

While the previously mentioned floor vote in 2011 saw Boehner receive unanimous Republican support, cracks had begun to emerge by the time he stood for reelection to the post in January 2013.

The year prior, a number of rebellious conservatives were stripped of their committee assignments in an attempt by Boehner to assert control and party discipline ahead of critical upcoming negotiations with President Obama around the fiscal cliff.

"You want good things in Congress and to have a good career? Better play along nicely," a Republican aide remarked at the time.

But when his last-ditch negotiations with President Obama collapsed, Boehner was forced to schedule a vote on a compromise bill late into the night on New Year's Day 2013, one that ultimately passed but saw nearly two-thirds of House Republicans vote no, many of whom pointed to an increase in the top marginal tax rate as a violation of their pledge to not raise taxes.

Days later, when the 113th Congress convened, Boehner had to fight to win a second term as Speaker, overcoming a loosely organized coup attempt that saw a dozen House Republicans vote for other candidates or abstain from the vote in a sign of protest—the largest number of defections in a Speaker's election in over two decades and the first real attempt by the nascent Freedom Caucus to use the vote for Speaker as a point of leverage.

By the time opening day 2015 rolled around, those defections had doubled to twenty-five—a sizeable bloc that could have been enough to force a second ballot if a number of Democrats had not been conspicuously absent that same day to attend funeral services for the late New York Governor Mario Cuomo. This fortuitous scheduling conflict was reportedly blessed by then–Minority Leader Nancy Pelosi, who maintained a warm working relationship with Speaker Boehner.

In response, Boehner once again removed a number of conservatives who voted against him from their posts, including several members who sat on the influential House Rules Committee. At best, this proved to be a temporary solution. At worst, it further fanned the flames with the Freedom Caucus and set the stage for what came next.

By the summer of 2015, the bad blood between Boehner and his right flank had reached its boiling point.

* * *

That July, a second-term congressman from North Carolina named Mark Meadows drafted a two-page resolution that would forever change the face of the modern speakership: a "Motion to Vacate."

First created by Speaker Joseph Cannon in 1910 as a means to call the bluff of his own rebellious detractors, a Motion to Vacate would—if adopted—remove the sitting Speaker from their position and automatically trigger a new election for the post.

Yet while Cannon gambled correctly that his dissatisfied colleagues were not careless enough to risk allowing the Speaker's gavel to fall into the other party's hands, we would have no such luck with the type of members we found ourselves dealing with over a century later.

Meadows—who famously fell to his knees to beg for Boehner's forgiveness following the 2013 coup attempt—now felt no such remorse about moving against the Ohioan. Instead, he itemized a number of grievances in his resolution, including claims that the Speaker had "endeavored to consolidate power and centralize decision-making" and had punished Members "who vote according to their conscience instead of the will of the Speaker."

The resolution concluded: "Whereas the House of Representatives, to function effectively in the service of all citizens of this country, requires the service of a Speaker who will endeavor to follow an orderly and inclusive process without imposing his or her will upon any Member thereof: Now, therefore, be it resolved that the office of Speaker of the House of Representatives is hereby declared to be vacant."

Instantly, the once obscure and arcane procedural mechanism became a rallying cry for the right. The August district work period became dominated by members facing questions in their town hall meetings on whether or not they supported the Speaker—a man who you might say was less than beloved by the grassroots at that point in time.

Eventually, and despite receiving signals from then–Minority Leader Nancy Pelosi that enough Democrats could be counted upon to vote present to allow him to keep the gavel, Speaker Boehner chose to step aside rather than put his colleagues through another contentious floor vote.

"It's become clear to me that the prolonged leadership turmoil would do irreparable harm to the institution," he told the press.

Inside the stunned conference meeting, Boehner followed his announcement by leading our members in reciting the prayer of Saint Francis: "Lord, make me an instrument of thy peace. Where there is hatred, let me sow love. . . . For it is in giving that we receive; it is in pardoning that we are pardoned; and it is in dying that we are born to eternal life."

* * *

Ironically, the day prior to his surprise announcement may have very well been one of Boehner's best days in the job. The Speaker had tried for years to invite a Pope to Congress, himself having grown up an altar boy in a Catholic family of twelve children. He finally succeeded in this mission when Pope Francis of the Holy See accepted his invite to address a Joint Meeting, the first such address ever given by a pontiff.

While I didn't shed quite as many tears as Speaker Boehner, the day of the Pope's address was a profoundly moving one for myself as a lifelong Catholic, as well—my most memorable experience as a Hill staffer to that point. As a member of the floor team, I was one of the few staffers allowed to be inside the House chamber for Pope Francis's remarks, which were delivered from the same podium where the president gives the annual State of the Union address.

The room was abuzz with anticipation, with no one quite certain what to expect from the Argentinian-born Pope who had only recently learned English for the purpose of his visit to the United States. Any nervousness quickly dissipated, however, when the Pope thanked the Speaker for extending him an invite to speak "in the land of the free and the home of the brave," a line that instantly brought the chamber to its feet in applause.

Even the justices of the Supreme Court—who traditionally refrain from shows of approval or disapproval during joint meetings—rose and joined in the ovation.

Pope Francis referenced the Golden Rule—"Do unto others as you would have them do unto you"—and framed it in terms of the issues of the day.

"If you seek security, provide security," he calmly stated. "If you want opportunity, give opportunity."

It was a powerful address, followed by the Pope taking to the Speaker's balcony for a public audience with a crowd of nearly fifty thousand that had begun gathering on the West Front of the Capitol as early as 4 a.m.

One of my coworkers on the communications team, Matt Sparks, brought his wife and their newborn daughter to the Capitol that day to be in the presence of the Pope. I felt bad that we were not able to get him a floor pass to attend the address in person, but Sparks reassured us that it was fine and that they would get seats on the West Front for the audience instead.

As fate would have it, the Pope began his blessing by thanking *"las personas mas importantes—los niños"*—or "the most important people, the children!" As he did so, he looked down into the crowd and saw Sparks holding his daughter up in the air. Both Kevin and Pope Francis immediately spotted them, and the Pope extended his hand outward to them for a blessing. A photographer captured that exact moment in a still shot that I am sure remains treasured in the Sparks household.

All in all, it was a joyous day for everyone at the Capitol—with no expectation whatsoever of what would follow just a day later.

* * *

At his final press conference, Speaker Boehner was asked if the Pope's visit affected his decision. Boehner demurred and largely said he had been planning to resign for some time but was simply waiting for the right opportunity.

"If you ask me, though, I definitely think it played a role," I noted in my journal that evening.

"Here was a man who worked in a largely thankless job day after day, while constantly hearing he wasn't good enough (and probably much worse too). And he was in the presence of a man not all that much older than him who was so clearly at peace. Deep down, I think the Speaker knew he wanted his life to be more like that and less how it currently was."

Months later, Boehner told the story of a curious question that was posed to him by John Dickerson of CBS during a *Face the Nation* appearance he made after the announcement.

"Do you think the power of the Holy Spirit brought you to this decision?" Dickerson asked.

While Boehner once again deflected during the interview, he admitted that the question remained on his mind.

"I thought about it Sunday, I thought about it Monday, I thought about it Tuesday. And then on Wednesday, Cardinal Wuerl came to see me"—the then-Cardinal for the Archdiocese of Washington, DC.

Boehner asked the Cardinal what he should make of the question and its nagging persistence on his mind.

"Well, John, you know we don't normally recognize the power of the Holy Spirit *except in retrospect*," the Cardinal offered, an observation that apparently struck a chord with Speaker.

"Instantly, all the dots lined up," Boehner stated, a moment of personal clarity that served as a fitting coda to a long career in public service.

* * *

While the dots were lining up for the outgoing Speaker, the dots also seemed to be lining up for Kevin. Another sudden, surprise leadership election was slated to take place in the coming weeks, and Kevin was already the early favorite to win, thanks in large part to the reservoir of chits he had built up among the membership through successive stints as chief deputy whip, majority whip, and majority leader.

As Speaker, Kevin would be responsible for guiding not only the Republican conference but the entire House of Representatives. The job also required dealing with the Senate—or the "country club," as Kevin called it in comparison to the "truck stop diner" of the House—as well as negotiating with the President of the United States. This is in addition to managing a hostile national press corps, recruiting and funding new candidates for office, rallying supporters across the country, and working to win more elections—all at the same time.

Once again, our floor team's vote-counting operation was up and running shortly after Boehner's announcement, and a letter that I drafted went out the following Tuesday to all of our members to officially declare Kevin's candidacy.

It touched upon everything our conference had been through together, from taking back the House in overwhelming fashion in 2010 to now nearly coming apart at the seams over deciding who should lead the party.

"We can't ignore the differences that exist, but we can and must heal the divisions in our conference with work, time, and trust," Kevin wrote. "That is why I have decided to run for Speaker of the House and graciously ask for your support."

The letter also proposed a more inclusive approach to governing than the tit-for-tat warfare that had characterized the relationship between Speaker Boehner and the Freedom Caucus.

> I am running to be your Speaker because I know that the People's House works best when the leadership you elect listens to members and respects the legislative process entrusted to committees. In short, I am guided by something Ronald Reagan once said: "The greatest leader is not necessarily the one who does the greatest things. He is the one that gets the people to do the greatest things."

* * *

That night, I summed up my thoughts in my journal.

"These races are always tricky and you never quite know what folks are up to," I wrote. "Hopefully, Kevin can win and exude the optimism and joy that Pope Francis did."

For good measure, I concluded the entry with a note of caution: "Time will tell. Never a dull moment."

While I hedged a little bit in my notes there, I would be lying if I were to say we were anything but confident at that point. Kevin was the only viable candidate running for the position, and we had successfully executed a similar shock-and-awe playbook only a year prior to win the position of majority leader.

On paper, we had the skills, the goodwill, and the know-how to get it done. All of the trips Kevin had taken with members, the fundraising visits to their districts, the early mornings in the gym, the late-night dinners, the amendments we helped get adopted, the bills we pushed over the finish line—they were adding up at just the right moment.

Put differently, the man who started his career by winning the lottery now seemed poised to hit another jackpot—and we assumed we were prepared to seize the opportunity.

We were wrong.

CHAPTER 5

FAILURE TO LAUNCH

"We are getting crushed right now," Matt Sparks said to me bluntly from his desk in our communications shop.

It was a fair assessment. Right out of the gate, Kevin did a ton of press—more than ever before. Multiple morning shows, followed by cable hits in the afternoon, then Fox News at night—all in just the day after announcing his candidacy.

Particularly in those years, I think even Kevin would admit that his words could bunch together on occasion. He joked that in first grade, he was one of ten students in the speech pathology class. In third grade, there were five. And by fifth grade, he had his own private tutor.

I caught parts of a CNN interview he did that day that veered into discussions of Hillary Clinton's slumping poll numbers in conjunction with the work of the Benghazi Select Committee—the panel that had recently uncovered Clinton's infamous use of a private server while serving as Secretary of State.

I understood what Kevin was trying to get at: Select committees could be powerful tools for uncovering the truth, and a similar strategy could be used to investigate other matters that were important to conservatives, such as the bombshell allegations roiling our conference at that time that Planned Parenthood was performing late-term abortions.

Nevertheless, the way it was worded came awfully close to making the work of the select committee sound political with regard to Clinton, the front-runner at the time for the Democratic nomination for president.

* * *

Although Kevin's CNN comments were not covered widely, we unfortunately chose to double down on this talking point that evening on Sean Hannity's program.

In 2015, Hannity was the single most dominant personality in the Fox News prime-time lineup. He had been a vocal antagonist of Speaker Boehner and an enthusiastic cheerleader for the aggressive shutdown tactics that Tea Party members like Texas Senator Ted Cruz were championing. Quite simply, his interviews and monologues could make or break any given Republican's standing with a very angry GOP base now well into the second term of President Obama.

While our internal vote count was strong and growing, the most frequent question we had to contend with was how Kevin would be different from Boehner. Hecklers sold McBOEHNER T-shirts at the Capitol South metro station, featuring an orange-tanned likeness of Kevin swirling Boehner's signature glass of merlot in one hand with a cigarette in the other—particularly ironic given that Kevin didn't drink or smoke.

Beneath the surface, the differences were obvious to those of us who had seen the two of them in action. Whereas Boehner's most-used nickname for members was jokingly "asshole," Kevin called anyone and everyone "sunshine."

Boehner relished his role as a Washington insider, his Speaker's office being a literal smoke-filled room from his constant chain-smoking. We staff could usually tell how good or bad a week was in store based upon how intense the cigarette smell was in the Republican cloakroom off the back of the House floor.

In fact, Boehner once confined a few holdouts on a major piece of legislation inside the Speaker's office, telling them they were free to leave when they were ready to vote yes and warning that he had "enough wine and cigarettes to last all night."

Kevin, on the other hand, dealt with the pressures of the job through daily workouts in the House gym or early-morning bike rides with other members around Washington, DC. It seemed to me that this was one of his best-kept secrets as far as getting the latest Hill gossip and keeping his finger on the pulse of the conference.

Finally, while Boehner deployed more of a stick approach in his later years, the results were decidedly mixed, with some members losing their reelection bids but others only becoming more influential and defiant in their martyrdom. Indeed, these strong-arm tactics were cited in the Meadows resolution as one of the grounds for Boehner's removal and in many ways led to the schism inside our conference from which the House Freedom Caucus was born.

In contrast, Kevin's view was that "you catch more flies with honey than vinegar." He believed that if you gave people a seat at the table and a window into the decision-making process, they might not always agree with your final play call, but at least they would understand it and be more willing to give it a chance.

Unfortunately for us, Hannity was not interested in members getting along and playing nice. Instead, the fateful two words of advice that were put into Kevin's ear before that interview were to "be angry"—advice that was in line with what the base wanted to see, but advice that worked against every one of Kevin's naturally optimistic instincts.

Not surprisingly, that mindset—combined with more than a little growing stress and fatigue—made for a bad interview.

* * *

"Sixty percent of Republicans polled this week feel betrayed by the Republican Party in Washington. Are they justified?" Hannity asked to kick off the interview. "I'm one of them."

Kevin certainly came across as ready to fight, maintaining a deathly serious demeanor and remarking that he was also frustrated by the lack of action on such measures as repealing Obamacare and overturning President Obama's Iran nuclear agreement.

For those of us watching at home, though, it was an unnatural posture for Kevin, and the interview slowly devolved into an interrogation.

After being repeatedly pushed by Hannity to move further and further to the right, Kevin tried to offer up a question on his own accord.

"The question I really think you wanna ask me is: How am I gonna be different?" Kevin said.

"I love how you ask my questions," Hannity smiled. "But go ahead, that was one of my questions"

Kevin let out a chuckle, briefly dropping his anger for a moment—only to then utter those fateful words.

"What you're gonna see is a conservative Speaker that takes a conservative Congress that puts a strategy in to fight and win," he began. "And let me give you one example."

A few McCarthy staffers and I have heard the next soundbite played so many times that we could rehearse it in our sleep. It is seared into our collective memories, marking the beginning of the end in 2015.

"Everyone thought Hillary Clinton was unbeatable, right? But we put together a Benghazi special committee, a select committee. What are her numbers today? Her numbers are dropping. Why? Cause she's untrustable," he said. "But no one would have known any of that had happened had we not fought and made that happen."

"I agree, that's something good, I give you credit for that," Hannity replied, ironically the only praise he offered over the entire course of the interview.

* * *

If Kevin received a relative pass for his CNN remarks, the remarks on *Hannity* set off a full-blown five-alarm shitstorm. The Curse of the Majority Leader had struck again.

Democrats used the comments to deflect from Clinton's persistent email woes and validate their suspicion that the select committee was yet another instance of "the vast right-wing conspiracy" that existed to harass the Clinton family and damage Hillary's quest for the presidency. They even offered legislation to dissolve the committee, citing Kevin's comments as the grounds for their motion.

On the Republican side, pundits decried it as giving Clinton the biggest break her campaign had seen in months—a charge that Kevin, the political animal, took as hard as any of the other criticisms.

Our detractors, thus far content to silently lie in wait, seized on the remarks as their chance to voice opposition to Kevin's candidacy—members like Tim Huelskamp of Kansas and Thomas Massie of Kentucky who now felt even more emboldened after having nudged John Boehner out of the Speaker's chair.

Most troublesome, the interview provided an opening for a high-profile challenger to emerge—someone not from the fringe, but from Kevin's own chairman's table: Jason Chaffetz of Utah, Chair of the House Committee on Oversight and Government Reform.

* * *

In the years prior, Chaffetz and Kevin had been fairly good friends.

The clean-cut Mormon Chaffetz was a regular presence on Fox News and the tip of the spear on multiple high-profile investigations into the Obama administration. Years later, he would become a more permanent fixture on the channel, leaving the House in 2017 to become a full-time Fox commentator—his boost in name recognition undoubtedly a result of his 2015 crusade against Kevin.

Chaffetz first emerged on our radar earlier that week when he began floating Trey Gowdy of South Carolina for the majority leader position that would presumably become open if Kevin were to become Speaker—a seemingly innocuous suggestion on its face, but also a noticeable sidestep from endorsing us.

In the aftermath of the Benghazi gaffe, however, Chaffetz went after Kevin more directly, calling the comments "absolutely inappropriate" and saying that Kevin should apologize immediately—which we attempted to do the next evening on Bret Baier's Fox program.

"This committee was set up for one sole purpose: to find the truth on behalf of families for four dead Americans," Kevin told Baier during an in-person prime-time interview.

But while Kevin had delivered the on-air apology and cleanup that proper Washington was clamoring for, the damage had been done. If anything, rather than assuaging concerns, it simply invited more—and prompted Chaffetz to announce his own long-shot candidacy for Speaker.

* * *

Making the rounds on that weekend's Sunday shows, Chaffetz touted himself as a "fresh face" who would represent a break from the leadership team that had overseen a worsening divide in our conference. He boasted of his ability to "articulate" a vision—a not-so-subtle jab. And in case that wasn't on the nose enough, he added "we need a Speaker who can speak."

Back on the Hill, the closed-door election among House Republicans to settle on a nominee for Speaker was only four days away, and Kevin's prospect of securing this vote of confidence from his colleagues was still on track. Our whip check showed Kevin north of 200 commitments before Chaffetz declared, and it was implausible that Chaffetz could significantly chip away at Kevin's strong internal support.

Unlike running for majority leader, however, being elected Speaker of the House was a two-step process. First was the secret-ballot vote that took place among party members to elect a "Speaker-designee." That was the easy part, with only a simple majority needed—which translated to 125 votes out of our 248 voting members at that time.

The more challenging part came on the floor, with the Speaker of the House needing 218 votes, or a majority of all House members present and voting. That translated to needing almost 90 percent of House Republicans at the time, an almost nonexistent margin for error.

It was here that Chaffetz attempted to throw sand in the gears, claiming that there were "up to fifty" members who could not or would not vote for a current member of leadership and that it was time to look for someone who could garner the requisite 218 floor votes—a.k.a. himself.

Once again, the Freedom Caucus began to smell blood in the water. And with time, the group sent unmistakable signals both in public and private that they were indeed intent on blocking Kevin's path on the floor.

"Several of my colleagues have commented that Jason [Chaffetz] has great qualities that would make him a good Speaker," Mark Meadows, leader of the anti-Boehner effort, told *The Washington Post*.

* * *

In the days leading up to the conference vote, I could see the inner turmoil in Kevin. His ever-present sunny disposition and glass-half-full demeanor gave way to something decidedly more downcast. He mused in private with us about the wisdom of simply remaining in his post as majority leader.

"If being Speaker is going to feel like this," he remarked, "then I'm not sure I want to be the Speaker."

On top of it all, a major government funding deadline was right around the corner, as well as the November 3 target date to raise the debt limit—a one-two punch that was among the most difficult challenges for any Republican Speaker to navigate, even in the best of circumstances.

Personally, I felt that we had no choice but to go for it. Who could say if the opportunity would ever present itself again? And while trying and failing is one thing, being stuck with the idea of what could have been could drive a person mad.

The newly emerging hangers-on and outside voices didn't help things either. A funny thing happens when you are on the verge of getting a promotion in Washington: Suddenly, everyone wants to be your best friend.

While one of Kevin's greatest qualities was his ability to bring people together and hear from a diverse range of opinions, this was something entirely different. In fact, it was downright maddening at times, with a free flow of well-wishers acting as if they were longtime senior advisers.

I had to get up and leave one such meeting in our conference room when a few outside counselors decided to take the lead on spitballing a strategy for how Kevin should approach a critical upcoming meeting with a group of holdouts. The only problem was that these supposed "gurus" couldn't even pick our detractors out of a lineup or name what their gripes were.

"Tell me, what state is Thomas Massie from?" I asked in a fit of anger, only to receive a wall of blank stares back.

Eventually, it was Judy McCarthy, Kevin's wife, who laid down the hammer.

"No more," she said. "That room is not good for him."

In a brief aside, I thanked her for speaking up. Apparently, the well-meaning but completely brain-dead outside advisers were driving her crazy too.

* * *

The morning of the internal party vote, I was anxious but had no reason to feel particularly nervous. That is, until my immediate boss, John Stipicevic—or "Stip"—walked back to our small section of the office.

Stip was Kevin's floor director, the keeper of the whip checks and the man in charge of knowing how all members planned to vote on each and every major initiative, including the upcoming leadership election. As a child, his parents said that he watched the House floor on C-SPAN rather than cartoons—and his seriousness and professionalism were qualities I looked up to and tried to emulate. But I could immediately tell something was off when Stip closed the door behind him and took a deep breath.

"Guys, we're going to drop out," he said.

Our three-person team responded only with stunned silence.

"There's nothing anyone here did wrong," he continued. "But this is the right decision."

The clock read 11:52 a.m., mere minutes before the Republican conference meeting was set to commence. Only a few hours before, we had prepped Kevin for a question-and-answer session with our membership that, by all accounts, went extremely well. Kevin even spent an hour with the Bakersfield Honor Flight group of World War II and Vietnam veterans and gave them a private floor tour—one of his favorite activities as a member and one of my favorite events to volunteer for as a staffer. In retrospect, it made sense that he was so at ease during this extended visit knowing something the rest of us did not.

While Stip relayed that we were north of the 218 commitments needed to win on the floor, he also shared that member after member told Kevin that voting for him would be a tough vote to address back home, particularly with an increasingly restless Republican base still worked up to a frenzy after Boehner's departure. And although most members said they would be willing to take the vote out of loyalty, Kevin was not comfortable making his friends put their necks on the line for him, especially if doing so could cause them to lose their primary election to an even crazier member. Instead, he would fall on the sword himself.

* * *

Just before noon, Kevin walked to the Longworth House Office building across the street from the Capitol and entered the cavernous Ways and Means Committee hearing room. There, as members began to file in and take their seats, Kevin asked to be recognized for a point of personal privilege.

Murmurs began to fill the room as confused members wondered aloud what might be occurring.

Kevin began by telling the members that he did not want to put the party through another slugfest just for his own sake. Instead, he said that it would be better if a new face took the helm at that time. And so for the good of the conference, he would be withdrawing his name from nomination for the position of Speaker of the House.

Members gasped. Suddenly, the meeting they had walked into only minutes prior with the expectation of choosing a new leader had now abruptly adjourned with no clear direction on the path forward.

"I think I shocked some of you, huh?" Kevin said at a press conference immediately following the confab.

"We should put this conference first," he added. "And I think there's something to be said for us to unite, we probably need a fresh face."

Members were not only stunned but exasperated at the inability of House Republicans to move forward as one.

"We can't go on like this where one small group is allowed to hijack the entire House," lamented moderate Pete King of New York.

Meanwhile, members of the Freedom Caucus could barely hide their glee.

"It's about changing the process," Mark Meadows told the press after the announcement, doing his best to conceal the knife that had now claimed not only Boehner, but Kevin, as well.

Another prominent individual on the right also took a victory lap following Kevin's decision to drop out: the newly ascendant leading candidate for the 2016 Republican presidential nomination, Donald Trump.

"They're giving me a lot of credit for that because I said you really need someone very, very, tough and very smart," Trump told a campaign rally in Las Vegas that day.

Between Cantor's defeat, the resignation of Speaker Boehner, and now Kevin's withdrawal from the race, the score for those keeping track at home was them 3, us 0.

* * *

On October 29, 2015, Paul D. Ryan of Wisconsin was elected the 54th Speaker of the House, the result of a weekslong persuasion campaign to draft him into the race.

Ryan lost nine Republican votes, while Daniel Webster of Florida—the Freedom Caucus' stalking horse—voted present. Not a unanimous vote, but as close to it as anyone could have hoped for under the circumstances.

Of course, Paul Ryan was a completely unique player inside the conference, someone who enjoyed rarefied air and DC-celebrity status following his selection as Mitt Romney's running mate in the 2012 presidential election. Patrick McHenry of North Carolina affectionately referred to him as "LBJ," or "Little Baby Jesus," a nod to the near-reverential awe he inspired among our members.

A self-described Jack Kemp Republican, policy wonk, and author of the Pathway to Prosperity budget proposals, Ryan was a darling of the fiscal hawks and think tank types. In addition, he made clear that he "didn't ask for this job," a statement of truth that both played well and seemed to create a "want what you can't have" effect. In fact, I started to believe it was perhaps the only way you could be elected Speaker in this modern Republican Party—if you actively ran not for the office, but away from it.

Initially, Ryan pledged only to run if he achieved the endorsement of all the major caucuses. He also declared to do away with the Motion to Vacate entirely. Many saw both stipulations as unattainable, an escape hatch for him to point to when they went unmet so that he could stay in his current position—chairman of the House Ways and Means Committee—while keeping his favorability numbers intact in case the former VP nominee were to mount his own run for president down the line.

With some time, however, and an extra dose of Catholic guilt from outgoing Speaker Boehner, Ryan came off of both demands slightly. While he didn't receive the 80 percent threshold required in the internal Freedom Caucus vote to establish "an official binding position," it was reported that he received the support of a supermajority of the conservative group—more than enough to put him over 218 votes on the floor in conjunction with the rest of the Republican conference.

Likewise, he punted on pursuing any changes to the Motion to Vacate until the start of the next Congress, when a new rules package would be debated. In private, though, he received handshake assurances from the Freedom Caucus that they would never bring such a vote against him.

The final big factor that worked in his favor was the calendar. Whereas Kevin would have needed to weather three weeks of attacks between the internal conference vote and the floor vote set to occur on the date of Boehner's resignation, by the time Ryan was finally talked into running for the job, there was only one day between the conference vote and the floor vote. Weeks of uncertainty and chaos had taken its toll—and our exhausted conference was ready to move forward.

* * *

Looking back, this was by far the toughest period of time to reflect upon and write about.

Don't get me wrong; if anyone had to win besides Kevin, we were glad it was a fellow Young Gun in Paul Ryan. We all expected that he would do a great job in the role. But hearing each member, one by one, call out the name "Ryan," I couldn't help but imagining them saying another last name.

Kevin came back and talked to a few of us in the floor office after the vote. He expressed a similar sentiment. For him, the hardest moment—a moment that also struck me—was when Ryan's wife and kids were recognized during his opening remarks and applauded by all the members of the House. That could have easily been Judy and the McCarthy children, and Kevin wondered aloud if he let them down.

"Maybe I missed my moment," he said.

While we agreed that he could have won, we tried to reassure him that there could always be another go around. At worst, being majority leader with one of your best friends as Speaker was not a bad consolation prize. And Ryan would frequently lean on Kevin for help understanding the conference dynamics, the ins and outs of the leadership table, and everything else that went into running the House.

But Kevin countered, "Timing is everything."

Up to that point, he had gotten to where he had in life by seizing an opportunity when it presented itself. Now, for the first time, a door opened and he wasn't able to jump through.

To add insult to injury, the day before Ryan's election, Boehner made good on his promise to "clean out the barn"—passing a two-year budget caps deal that funded the government and raised the debt limit, erasing the two major roadblocks that we had so agonized over in one fell swoop. That left the new Speaker with a clear track of runway to operate from, while Boehner happily took all the arrows on his way out the door and the Freedom Caucus looked on powerlessly.

* * *

"Time will tell if our moment comes again," I recorded in my journal that evening.

After all, it did for Boehner, who was ousted from a prior leadership role as conference chair in the late 1990s, went on to serve as chair of the committee on Education and the Workforce, and eventually worked his way back to the top.

Inside the chattering class, however, Washington largely doubted Kevin's appetite to serve indefinitely in what amounted to a political purgatory. Pundits and lobbyists openly mused that he was merely putting on a brave face, only to have his eyes on an exit of his own. In fact, a colleague who I greatly respected called and told me in no uncertain terms that *The Washington Post* was going to publish a story the following week reporting that Kevin was planning to resign from Congress.

"As a friend, I wanted to give you a heads-up so that you could make alternative arrangements," he told me.

While that story never ran, it is no exaggeration to say that DC had already drafted Kevin's political obituary and was ready to hit send at a moment's notice.

But for myself and a few loyal McCarthy staffers, leaving never once crossed our minds.

Perhaps we were bonded by the experience, having learned much more in defeat than we ever would have in victory.

"The greatest teacher, failure is," as Yoda would say.

Whatever it was, we came back more determined than ever to prove the doubters wrong.

"It's not whether you get knocked down," Kevin would often remind us. "The question is can you come back?"

We weren't sure how long it might be or if there even would be another next time. We certainly did not anticipate all that would transpire in between—including the biggest jolt to the American political system of our lifetimes, the 2016 election of Donald Trump as president. Nor could we have foreseen the rise of a new class of House members who would make our former foes look downright tame by comparison.

But through it all, our tight-knit team hung together. Rebuilt what was broken. Fortified areas of weakness. Strengthened our relationships, inside and outside the building. Sharpened our instincts. Held the party together during some truly turbulent times. And we waited.

It would be seven long years until opportunity knocked again.

PART II
BATTLE LINES

CHAPTER 6

A NIGHT TO FORGET

Heading into the 2022 midterm elections, it seemed like the stars were finally aligning for Team McCarthy.

That year's off-year elections—traditionally a harbinger for the cycle—both broke strongly Republican, just as they had in 2009 before the Tea Party blowout. Businessman Glenn Youngkin defeated Terry McAuliffe in the race for the Virginia governorship, an office that McAuliffe had previously held in a commonwealth that Joe Biden carried by nearly ten points only a year prior. Likewise, in New Jersey, an even bluer state that voted for Biden by over fifteen points in 2020, Republicans came within a few thousand votes of knocking off incumbent Governor Phil Murphy.

Inflation raged throughout the economy, with the price of gas, food, and housing up nearly 10 percent from the previous year—a by-product of the unprecedented spending spree undertaken during the COVID-19 pandemic that was further exacerbated by President Biden's so-called Inflation Reduction Act.

Taken together, Washington was openly predicting another Red Wave that would be more than enough to propel Republicans back into the House majority and provide a buffer for Kevin—then serving in his second term as House minority leader—to become Speaker with a handful of defections to spare.

Motivated as ever, Kevin spent the cycle raising a record $500 million for Republican campaign efforts, traveling to nearly every state in the union, and enlisting more Republican women, minorities, and veterans to run for

Congress than at any time in modern history. From Juan Ciscomani in Arizona and John James in Michigan to Jen Kiggans in Virginia, Erin Houchin in Indiana, Laurel Lee in Florida, and countless other top-tier recruits, we felt as though the wind was at our backs for the better part of 2022.

My career had also advanced in the intervening years as I gradually took on greater responsibilities in the office, from preparing Kevin for his weekly "colloquy" debates with Maryland Democrat Steny Hoyer to helping put together the slideshow presentations and talking points that Kevin would deliver at our weekly conference meetings and annual member retreats.*

"Chase skills and responsibility, not titles or salary," one of my mentors, James Min, once wisely counseled me. "If you do, the rest will follow."

He was right as these new assignments put me face-to-face with the boss and helped me better understand how Kevin and our conference thought, anticipate what they wanted to do, and figure out how to get it done—three skills that would come to define my role in the office moving forward.

Of course, timing mattered quite a bit for Hill staffers, as well. Every two years, we would brace for the election, knowing our fortunes could rise or fall in an instant based upon the results.

To prepare for this uncertainty, I was given a slightly different piece of advice—from former Vice President Dick Cheney, no less: "Hope for chaos."

"Watergate happened, everyone ran from the party," Cheney explained in a brief private aside we shared when I was a junior aide. "But I stayed and became the youngest White House chief of staff in history."

In that regard, the years leading up to 2022 featured plenty of upheaval, including Donald Trump's surprise victory returning Republicans to the White House after a long eight-year hiatus.

This changing of the guard opened vast new opportunities for Republican staffers looking to make the jump to the Executive Branch. One such aide was

---

* My personal favorite was a member retreat slideshow that Kevin asked us to model on Hans Rosling's viral TED Talk, "The Best Stats You've Ever Seen." Complete with moving, color-coded dots of different shapes and sizes, it was unlike any presentation our members had seen before—officially ending the Republican era of PowerPoints that consisted of nothing but black text bullet points on a white background.

my direct boss at the time, Ben Howard, who accepted a senior role in Trump's Office of Legislative Affairs. His departure, in turn, created a vacancy for the position of Kevin's floor director, the job I had most aspired to since I first interned on Capitol Hill.

As you might imagine, it was not a long conversation when Kevin pulled me into his office to offer the job, making me the youngest Republican floor director in history at the ripe old age of twenty-five and elevating me into his innermost circle of trusted senior staff.

That same year, I also met a young clerk for the Energy and Commerce Committee named Giulia Giannangeli at Speaker Paul Ryan's Christmas party. We hit it off immediately and gradually fell in love, a classic Hill romance. I proposed to her on the eastern shore of Saint Michaels, Maryland in October 2020, and we were married a year later at St. Joseph's Catholic Church on Capitol Hill in a beautiful ceremony attended by our family, friends, and colleagues.

* * *

Only two short years after Trump's election, Republicans lost the House and found ourselves in the minority.

I can confidently say that working in the minority was easily my least favorite job in Washington, consisting largely of conjuring up activities to keep our restless members busy since they were otherwise legislatively powerless.

The minority did create some interesting new dynamics, however, with formerly bitter enemies in the party now suddenly unified in fighting against Nancy Pelosi and the Democratic majority. One such improbable alliance that formed was between Kevin and Ohio Representative Jim Jordan.

It is difficult to overstate how dramatic of a turnaround occurred between these two lawmakers. Originally elected together in the class of 2006, Kevin and Jim came into Congress as friends, only to slowly take divergent paths in the House.

While Kevin ascended the leadership ladder, Jim made a name for himself by lobbing bombs at the members of leadership, cofounding the House Freedom Caucus and serving as its chair from 2015 to 2017 before handing the torch to his friend Mark Meadows. Jordan even ran against Kevin for the position of minority leader in 2018 in a hard-fought campaign.

Nevertheless, Kevin always respected Jim's talents and work ethic and felt that the two men would be stronger working together than against one another. And so, over some very loud initial objections from the Republican Steering Committee, Kevin vouched for his onetime antagonist to be the lead Republican on multiple key panels—first Oversight, then Judiciary—roles in which Jim excelled and that allowed him to experience firsthand the pressures that Kevin and the leadership team faced on a daily basis.

A few years later, Kevin cemented another influential ally on the emerging New Right: freshman firebrand Marjorie Taylor Greene of Georgia. As with Jim, Kevin saw that Marjorie was someone who innately understood the rapidly changing base of the Republican Party.

"She knows what she's doing," Kevin later said. "You've got AOC and MTG,"—referring to the other freshman lawmaker known by her three initials, New York progressive Alexandria Ocasio-Cortez.

Despite Marjorie coming into office in 2021 surrounded by a wave of controversy, Kevin aggressively fought back against Democrats' unprecedented move to remove her from her committee assignments, the first in a series of overtures that gradually won Marjorie over to our cause and helped transform her from a lightning rod to a strategic advocate.

"You are like a pitcher who throws a 100-mph fastball," I told her in one of our first conversations on the House floor. "You'll give up a lot of runs if you hit every batter. But you will be unstoppable if you can throw strikes."

Part of Kevin's outreach included inviting Marjorie to meetings and events that might have been previously reserved for more tenured members of the conference, such as the rollout of our Commitment to America agenda that would serve as House Republicans' policy platform for the 2022 midterms.

The night before the October rollout of the Commitment, Kevin convened a group of members across the ideological spectrum to break bread over an Italian dinner in Monongahela, Pennsylvania. Looking around the table, I marveled to myself at this gathering that would have been unfathomable only years earlier, with Jim Jordan and Marjorie Taylor Greene sitting alongside the members of our elected leadership team, sipping wine, talking, and smiling.

One by one, Kevin asked each member to go around the table and share an issue that they would like to be known for tackling during their time in Congress—a variation of his preferred icebreaker at large dinners, where he would ask guests to reveal their first concert or the three people in history they would most want to have a meal with.

While most members stated policy objectives like advancing school choice or strengthening America's national security, when it came to Representative Greene, she stated that her main goal was to unite the various factions of the Republican conference, put an end to the infighting, and make sure we trained our fire on the Democrats.

Stunned, moderate Ohio Representative Dave Joyce leaned over to me and asked, "How did you get her to say that?"

Indeed, over the months to come, both Jim and Marjorie would prove to be two of Kevin's fiercest defenders. They were joined by a chorus of outside conservative voices—ranging from Sean Hannity, Charlie Kirk, and Matthew Boyle to Mark Levin and Donald Trump Jr.—with whom Kevin had assiduously built relationships over the past seven years after we learned the hard way in 2015 what it felt like to have next to no air cover on our rightmost flank.

* * *

While the midterm outlook remained bright for Republicans and bleak for Democrats throughout most of 2022, that quickly changed in June when the US Supreme Court issued a landmark ruling that struck down *Roe v. Wade*.

All of a sudden, an election that we expected to be about the economy and the border—issues on which polls showed the public clearly favoring Republicans—became an election as much about abortion, health care, and social issues, with both opponents and supporters of abortion as fired up as they had ever been.

Maybe it was naiveté, but I still felt cautiously optimistic when I awoke on Election Day 2022, especially when compared to how I felt ahead of both the 2016 and 2020 elections—years when pundits had forecasted disaster for Republicans only for us to defy expectations.

For official-side, non-campaign staffers, there's not much to do on the day of an election besides doomscroll on social media and read too much into exit polls that mean absolutely nothing. So I did what I would normally do to take my mind off things: golf.

Two years prior, a few McCarthy staffers, including Matt Sparks, Drew Florio, Tim Monahan, and I, had begun an unofficial tradition of playing a round of golf on Election Day, with this year's match taking place at the course on the University of Maryland campus about fifteen miles north of Capitol Hill. To keep things interesting, we made up a game where prior to each hole, we would designate a state with a marquee Senate race. If anyone in the group scored a par on that hole, it would count as a Republican win. If not, it would count as a Democratic win.

We carded a par on the holes assigned to Wisconsin, Arizona, and North Carolina—but lost Georgia, Pennsylvania, and Nevada. Not exactly an encouraging start, especially since we were missing our best golfer, Drew Florio, that year.

After we were done ruining the Senate Republicans' chances, we decided to switch gears to the House. Any birdie would be a gain of ten seats, five seats for a par, one seat for a bogey, and minus five seats for a double bogey or worse. At the end of the round, we totaled up our scores and showed a net gain of only eight seats for House Republicans, an equally unfortunate outcome.

Lesson learned: Get better at golf.

* * *

That evening, my wife and I hosted a pre-party at our Navy Yard apartment for staff and friends to hang out before heading over to Kevin's official victory party downtown.

Perhaps it was the superstitious side of me carrying over from the round of golf, but I felt incredibly uneasy from the very start of the night.

What if every year we felt like we would lose, we won—and every year we felt like we would win, we lost? I asked myself.

As I nervously flipped back and forth from Fox to CNN to MSNBC, the initial returns coming in were somewhat positive. Florida was trending strongly in our direction. Likewise, Republicans were holding their own in three competitive races in nearby suburban Virginia. And New York Republicans were mounting a charge all across the Empire State, buoyed by former House member Lee Zeldin's anti-crime campaign for governor—including a race that saw the head of House Democrats' campaign arm, Sean Patrick Maloney, trailing Republican challenger Mike Lawler in the Hudson Valley.

As 9 p.m. approached and I continued to feel too nervous to sit still, I rallied the group to pack up and make our way over to the official festivities taking place in downtown DC at the Westin Hotel.

Unfortunately, things only went downhill on our drive to the hotel.

This was the congressional equivalent of "the witching hour"—where wins become losses and losses become wins. First, my Twitter feed showed Virginia Democrats slowly pulling back ahead. That news was followed by one of Kevin's favorite candidates of the cycle—Mayor Allen Fung in Rhode Island—also falling behind, a seat that Kevin had internally projected would be a win.

Rhode Island was always a reach anyways, I told myself. *Stay calm.*

As I worked my way through the hotel, the atmosphere felt like a carnival-style fun house, with room after room of music blaring, dimmed lights, throngs of media and inebriated supporters all milling around as if everything was fine. But when I entered Kevin's private "war room" on the second floor, it was very clear to me that all was not well.

* * *

Seated across the table from Kevin was former Speaker Newt Gingrich, along with his wife, Ambassador Callista Gingrich. Over the years, Newt had become close friends with Kevin, helping consult on a variety of projects, including the aforementioned Commitment to America agenda. Newt also joined Kevin on multiple trips across the country to stump for candidates throughout 2022, creating a powerful visual of the former Republican Speaker working alongside the future Republican Speaker.

Also at the table was Newt's former chief of staff, Dan Meyer, who was brought on in 2019 to serve as Kevin's chief of staff. A steady and experienced hand, Dan had worked at the highest levels in Washington for over four decades, including a stint as the top legislative affairs aide to former President George W. Bush before decamping for a career in the private sector. He was enjoying a more relaxed chapter in his life filled with golf and grandkids until Kevin called out of the blue and successfully convinced him to jump back into the arena for one last hurrah—a decision we were all grateful for.

The room was rounded out by Representative Jason Smith of Missouri, a future Chairman of the Ways and Means Committee, Kevin's political director and future Georgia Representative Brian Jack, Dan Conston of the Congressional Leadership Fund super PAC, Matt Sparks and Natalie Joyce from our official team, Kevin's close friend Jeff Miller, and a number of campaign aides circling in and out with the latest updates—each report worse than the last.

This is not good, I told myself, taking a healthy sip of bourbon.

Fed up, Kevin finally called Dave Wasserman of the *Cook Political Report* to inquire what he was seeing on the ground.

"I think I'm going to be calling you Mr. Minority Leader for another term," he said.

The side chatter fell silent.

"Huh? No," Kevin replied.

"Right now, our model has you winning 217 seats," Wasserman relayed. "Sorry, that's what I'm seeing."

Kevin hung up the phone and sent a jolt through the room. If the prospect of remaining in the minority wasn't real before, it was real now.

Adios, Red Wave.

* * *

In an instant, Kevin pushed out his chair and shuttled down the hall to the larger staff war room. There, a long rectangular table of over twenty campaign aides was assembled, the glow of laptop screens illuminating their concerned faces as they crunched and re-crunched the numbers. Along the walls in front of and behind them, multiple large flat screens updated in real time with district returns and projections from throughout the country.

One by one, Kevin began to grill the regional leads on each of their outstanding races, down to the towns and precincts that had ballots left to count.

"Are those Election Day or mail-in ballots left?" he asked.

"Election Day," an aide would reply.

"Okay, we'll take that one."

And so on and so forth. For once in my life, I was more than happy to literally melt into obscurity against the wall.

After about thirty minutes of this rapid-fire exercise, the political nerds assured Kevin that we would eventually surpass 218 seats, maybe even reach as many as 228 to 230. They reviewed the path at least a half dozen times until Kevin was satisfied that he could confidently count to 218—the bare minimum needed to claim a House majority.

While hitting 218 would indeed produce a majority on paper and was viewed by the political folks as a technical victory, our job on the official side had now become exponentially more difficult. Simply put, I could not imagine such a tight majority would be enough to elect Kevin—or anyone else for that matter—as Speaker of the House given the number of agitators we presumed would be all too eager to rerun their obstruction playbook from 2015.

* * *

A vigorous debate broke out behind the scenes on the question of whether Kevin should address the media and gathered supporters or not, with a vocal contingent on the political team arguing that Kevin should only speak after Republicans flipping the House became "official." By that point, however, the night had drawn into morning, and an official call could have still been hours, if not days, away.

Our communications director, Matt Sparks, and I grabbed Kevin's longtime deputy chief of staff, James Min, to argue our case.

James had been with Kevin longer than any other aide, tracing back to their days working together for former Representative Bill Thomas. More consigliere than staffer, James was the person who first hired me to work for Kevin as a junior-level aide and who I most looked up to for advice. He had seen it all before, and we trusted he would know what to do in that moment.

"We gotta get out there. Rally the troops. Have something for the news stations to show," Sparks and I argued.

"Mhm, I agree," James responded after carefully considering the options.

"And guess what? If we don't win the House, it's all over anyways," we said.

It is not hyperbole to say that Kevin had staked it all on winning the majority. Everything in his career had been building to this moment. But if we came up short this time, I did not sense an appetite for another stint in the minority. For Team McCarthy, this was truly now or never.

In haste, we drafted up a few simple talking points, marked them up with Kevin, and told him to get out there—chief among them, a declarative statement: "It is clear: we are going to take back the House." Meanwhile, the rest of our team attempted to wrangle up as many drunk bodies as possible to fill in the crowd and cheer so that the TV clips might look a bit more celebratory on the following day's broadcasts.

When Kevin finally took the stage with National Republican Congressional Committee Chair Tom Emmer and Republican National Committee Chair Ronna McDaniel, it was nearing 2 a.m.

"Thank you all very much. I know it's a late night," he began.

Earlier that week, there had been a discussion over what signs to hand out and what words to have on the backdrop, with us coming incredibly close to plastering "Ready to Deliver" on all these various walls and signs. Fortunately, at the last minute, we settled on the more generic, "Take Back the House"—avoiding our own "Dewey Defeats Truman" moment.

For good measure, Kevin ad-libbed a line not in the talkers.

"Now, let me tell you. You're out late. But when you wake up tomorrow, we will be in the majority and Nancy Pelosi will be in the minority!" he said, prompting a round of bleary-eyed applause.

If only that prediction had come true.

CHAPTER 7

OVERTIME

To quote boxing legend and modern-day philosopher Mike Tyson: "Everybody has a plan until they get punched in the face."

Our original plan was to win a dozen to twenty seats, project confidence, fly above the fray, and create a sense of inevitability. In fact, we had an entire choreography lined up to announce the creation of "transition teams" the day after the election to prepare for the majority.

The only issue, of course, was that on the morning of November 9, it still was not clear if there would be a majority to prepare a transition for. None of the major networks had called the House as being flipped, and it wasn't clear if or when that would occur.

Good political practice—as well as superstition—would dictate that you prepare both a victory speech and a concession speech before any election. But preparing to announce a run for House leadership was not as straightforward.

You could win big or win narrowly. Surpass expectations or fall short of expectations. Depending on whether it was a midterm or presidential, you had to account for your party's performance across the House, Senate, and White House and whether those were holds or pickups.

So in actuality, there could be about eight to ten different scenarios to account for—far too many to write complete draft letters for. Thus, my practice was to pick the most likely two or three scenarios and outline a letter for those outcomes. Unfortunately, I had a nasty streak of writing every letter except the one we would actually need.

In 2016, for instance, we prepared a draft that accounted for us keeping the House and another that assumed we kept the House and Senate. But considerably less time was spent on the one that contemplated Donald Trump winning the White House. That particular letter ended up being rewritten in a Bakersfield Four Points Sheraton hotel room at 2 a.m. over In-N-Out burgers, with Kevin relaying to the conference that he "just got off the phone with President-Elect Trump and Vice President-Elect Pence . . . [after a] historic night."

Likewise, in 2020, our draft letter anticipated us falling well short of taking back the House and attempted to frame the election as a valiant step forward in a longer battle to come. Instead, we vastly outperformed expectations, and Kevin's subsequent calls for support were a breeze with the rejuvenated members of our conference.

Needless to say, in 2022 there was not a letter that envisioned a scenario where the House majority remained uncalled. That resulted in more than a few lines ending up on the cutting-room floor, like: ~~"A red wave made landfall from sea to shining sea, from Rhode Island to Oregon..."~~

Instead: "This was the most expensive and arguably the most competitive House midterm in America's history. Yet in a hard-fought contest, our message and our candidates prevailed, winning key seats across the country, some in districts that President Biden carried just two years ago by double digits."

"While a number of races remain outstanding," it continued, "I can confidently report that we will build on our significant gains from last cycle and achieve our goal of taking back the House."

* * *

After sending out the announcement letter to our members—commonly referred to as a "Dear Colleague" for its boilerplate salutation—the next step was to lock down enough commitments to win the internal party vote that was set to take place roughly a week later to determine the party's "Speaker-designee."

As previously detailed, Kevin and our team had run and won multiple such leadership races over the past decade—thanks, in large part, to our familiarity with a closely guarded playbook that had been passed down through leadership staff for generations. Without revealing all of our secrets, this battle-tested blueprint was centered around three key maxims.

Maxim #1: Trust Your 1-to-5s

The first component and most critical piece of our strategy was what we internally referred to as the "One to Five" list (or "1-to-5"). This list assigned a numerical value to every member of the conference based on how likely or unlikely they would be to vote for us, with one being an absolute "yes" vote and five being an absolute "no" vote.

For the McCarthy office, our director of member services, Natalie Joyce, was the keeper of this highly confidential list, and no one did it better. A Mississippi dynamo, Natalie was a longtime member of the team, having been first recruited by Kevin when he was elected majority whip to serve as one of his top staff liaisons with the members. In this role, Natalie was responsible for tracking and helping deliver upon the multitude of hopes and dreams our members had for their time in Congress, from committee assignments and chairmanships to legislative and district priorities.

Over the course of the year, Natalie, our chief of staff, and I would schedule periodic check-ins with Kevin to diligently reevaluate the list from top to bottom. And in a very real way, the 1-to-5 list told its own story.

For example, let's say we just took a successful overseas trip with a member, elevated them to their committee of choice, or helped them move a high-priority bill. That might call for upgrading them from a three to a two, or a two to a one.

Conversely, if a member was mad at us for any given reason—they felt passed over for a committee assignment or snubbed by some other perceived slight—that could warrant flagging them for future outreach and perhaps even moving them down a category if the damage was severe enough.

More art than science, this living document was the foundation upon which all successful leadership races were built and served as a road map to unlock the next, equally important maxim.

Maxim #2: Speed Kills

Being the first to call other members and lock up their support early was the name of the game. In fact, a handful of members over the years would commit to whoever called them first, not knowing that other calls might still be coming. By the time any other challenger called to inquire, it was too late.

In most of Kevin's races, we aimed to secure a majority of the conference on Day 1, well before other potential candidates ever had a chance to determine if there was a lane for them. After all, "every battle is won before it's ever fought," and we aimed to use that to our advantage.

Time was our only finite asset. Therefore, while Kevin was busy making his own personal calls—which started with the largest and most crucial pool of 2s and 3s—we also deployed a deputy whip team of other members to make calls on his behalf.

Typically, this group was made up of anywhere from twenty to thirty whips known as "counter-callers."

To be chosen as a counter-caller, the member was not only a big supporter of our boss but also had experience whipping other members and represented a cross section of our conference, whether in terms of ideology, committee assignment, region, or terms of service. Some of our best counter-callers were Patrick McHenry of North Carolina, Guy Reschenthaler of Pennsylvania, Virginia Foxx of North Carolina, Dusty Johnson of South Dakota, Stephanie Bice of Oklahoma, and Kelly Armstrong of North Dakota, along with countless others who were well-respected, had deep relationships with the members, and generally kept a great feel for the pulse of the conference.

At the staff level, we would assign these deputies a list of names to call and provide a brief script outlining our candidate's vision. In turn, they would report back any relevant feedback, all of which would get inputted into our internal whip check and continually updated throughout the race. That brings us to the third maxim.

Maxim #3: Members—Not the Media—Vote for You

All too often, aspiring leadership candidates would fall into the trap of thinking the election was an outside game rather than an inside game. They would chase high-profile endorsements, splashy media pieces, or cable TV interviews thinking that was the route to win votes.

Instead, the exact opposite was true. Internal congressional races were almost exclusively about the member-to-member connection and how well you could build and solidify a relationship. Not a single Fox News host or Twitter personality held a vote, but the delegates and resident commissioners from Guam, Puerto Rico, and American Samoa did. We always kept that in mind and allocated our time accordingly.

In the same vein, it was important to hear what a member was saying, not what we wanted to hear. For example, a member saying "You would be great for this role" was most certainly *not* taken as an indication of their intention to vote for us.

In fact, unless a member explicitly told Kevin, "You have my support," we operated as if we did not have their support. And even if they did say they supported Kevin, some members would flat-out lie. To be safe, we accounted for up to a 10 percent error rate.

A word here to any members or staff reading this: If you plan to support the candidate asking for your vote, there is only one answer that is appreciated—a clear, unambiguous "Yes, of course you have my support." Even if you are lying, that should be your response.

Once, a somewhat senior member responded to Kevin's call in an uncontested race by saying, "Well, I guess I don't see why not. There's no one else running against you, right?" That was definitely not the correct answer, and an asterisk was now on their file for all the wrong reasons.

Conversely, the members who were really smart would proactively text Kevin and tell him to save his time calling them, that they were in our corner 100 percent.

* * *

On our kickoff call with the counter-callers in 2022, the energy was extremely positive. Members were excited to be going into the majority and helped to pump Kevin up. Despite the slog that was ahead, they were committed to seeing him elected Speaker.

The main questions that we encountered on our calls with the broader membership were (1) "Are we going to win?" and (2) "How big is our majority going to be?"

At that time, the political folks were still telling us that 226–228 was within the realm of possibility.

"It's like we won the Super Bowl, but in overtime," Kevin told member after member. "We're still champions; it's just going to take a little longer."

He also borrowed a line from our general counsel, Machalagh Carr: "They don't give out gavels in small, medium, or large—they just give you the gavel."

Those answers seemed to put members' minds at ease. And in general, the calls were going smoothly, a testament to the deep well of support Kevin had built up over years of dutifully serving the conference and grinding to win us the majority.

But as the week rolled on and our internal whip count continued to inch upward, the projections for the overall size of the majority continued to maddeningly inch downward.

On Thursday, we were told 226 was the absolute ceiling. By Friday, best case was 223–224.

How is this happening right now? I asked myself over and over.

* * *

Internally, we continued to do our best to block out the noise and stick to our strategy, making good progress with the 2s and 3s while sprinkling in a few calls to Freedom Caucus members, particularly incoming freshmen we expected might be joining the HFC.

Off the bat, those calls were going well too. Kevin secured quick commitments from numerous freshmen, including Mike Collins of Georgia and Cory Mills of Florida, two individuals who were somewhat skeptical of us at the start of their respective runs for Congress. But after a handful of calls, the Freedom Caucus began a clearly choreographed effort to duck our outreach.

Most simply stopped answering. Those brave enough to take Kevin's call repeated some form of: "Sorry, I just cannot commit yet."

Uh oh, I thought. *I do not like this.*

This avoidance was coupled with increasing statements from the Freedom Caucus to delay the coming internal leadership elections, a tried-and-true play in their repertoire and one that we had repeatedly beat back over the years.

This time, however, they actually had a decent case to make that we should not proceed until we knew Republicans actually had a majority.

"The rules of the game should be known before we select a captain," Freedom Caucus Chair Scott Perry said in an interview. "We don't know what the majority is or who is in the majority. It seems appropriate that we have a family conversation prior to voting."

As the top House Republican, Kevin technically had the final authority to set the date for the internal party elections. And unlike years past when we had outright dismissed the notion, we had a serious debate on the wisdom of delaying the internal leadership elections by a few days, which could serve to earn some goodwill with the Freedom Caucus.

Ultimately, we decided that it was impossible to know how long it could take for the networks to call the House majority and that waiting for an official declaration would only give more time for mischief to brew. This proved to be a wise decision as an official call was not made by the Associated Press until November 17, a full nine days after the midterms.

Final count: 222 Republicans and 213 Democrats.[*]

* * *

On paper, you are probably thinking there was a straightforward path to being elected Speaker with 222 Republicans. We merely had to keep our defections to four or fewer to gain the requisite 218 votes to be elected to the top job in the House.

But that Congress was anything but straightforward. Instead, only about 200 of our 222 Republicans truly saw themselves as part of the team. For the remaining twenty or so members—many of whom viewed themselves as Freedom Caucus first rather than Republican—it would be up to Kevin to convince them to form a coalition-style government with the rest of our party,

---

[*]   Prior to January, the number of House Democrats would decrease by one with the passing of Virginia Representative Don McEachin on November 28 after a battle with colorectal cancer.

a first in the modern House of Representatives and more akin to the parliamentary systems seen across Europe.

"I will be a listener every bit as much as a Speaker, striving to build consensus from the bottom up rather than commanding the agenda from the top down," Kevin stated in his introductory Dear Colleague letter to the conference. "Everyone has something valuable to bring to the table and my door will always be open to your ideas and input on how we best achieve our shared goals."

In a vacuum, this sentiment was genuine. Kevin's preferred leadership style was, as you have seen, more collaborative—built on bringing people in, hearing them out, and seeking to move forward as one.

But I would be lying if I said we were excited about just how much collaboration was about to be in store for us—and with who.

CHAPTER 8

THE OPPOSITION

From the jump, it was clear we were going to have a battle on our hands.

"I was praying each evening for a small majority because I recognized that that small majority was the only way that we were going to advance a conservative agenda," Matt Rosendale of Montana later admitted.

If that was the case, he and his brethren in the Freedom Caucus had gotten their wish.

From where we sat, there were two camps emerging among the group of holdouts: the Never Kevins and the Maybe Kevins, each with their own unique motivations and temperaments.

Camp 1: The Never Kevins

The Never Kevins were prepared to block Kevin's path to the speakership simply because they could—largely based upon personal vendettas and grievances. Simply put, this group smelled blood in the water and was prepared to hold out as long as they could.

Senator Tim Scott of South Carolina spoke with Kevin during one of our breaks from making member calls and compared our predicament with this group to that of two trucks speeding head-on at one another in a game of chicken.

"Do you know how you win a game of chicken, Kevin?" the South Carolinian asked. "You wait until you see the whites of their eyes. And then you throw the steering wheel out the window."

That became an accurate encapsulation of our approach to the Never Kevins, led by chief antagonist Matt Gaetz of Florida.

A carbon copy of the villain Syndrome from *The Incredibles* in both looks and demeanor, and raised in the house where Jim Carrey's character lived in *The Truman Show,* Matt Gaetz was the nepotism baby of former Florida state Senate President Don Gaetz. Described by one of his Democratic colleagues to the *New Yorker* as a "sociopath," I regret to inform you that his is a name that you will need to know moving forward.

For a period of time, it actually seemed plausible that Gaetz was on his way out of Congress, with *The New York Times* reporting in March 2021 that Gaetz was under investigation for the sexual assault of a seventeen-year-old. That same investigation led to the indictment of his former wingman Joel Greenberg on thirty-three counts, including sex trafficking crimes involving a minor.

Though Gaetz denied the accusations, the allegations made more sense when considering a peculiar request that Gaetz reportedly made at the end of President Trump's first term: a blanket pardon for himself.

Trump's White House lawyer Eric Herschmann later testified that "the pardon that [Gaetz] was discussing, requesting, was as broad as you could describe."

"I remember he said, from the beginning of time up until today—for any and all things," Herschmann detailed.

It was hard to pinpoint the origin of Gaetz's beef with Kevin. In Tallahassee, Gaetz fell somewhere between a moderate and a libertarian—even supporting Jeb Bush for president until he sensed the political winds shifting and became a full-fledged Trump supporter.

"You've got to have the ability to reinvent yourself in this game many times," Gaetz would later tell *The New York Times.*

In that regard, leading the crusade against Kevin in 2022 was a surefire way for Gaetz to boost his profile, get more cable TV hits, and be seen as "fighting"—just as it had been for Mark Meadows in 2015 against John Boehner.

To join his cause, Gaetz recruited freshman Representative Bob Good from Virginia—who we internally referred to as "Bob Bad" or "Bob Not Good."

Unceasingly frowning, Good was the unique politician who the more voters got to know him, the less they liked him. That held true inside Congress, as well, where he felt the need to speak at every meeting and possessed an uncanny ability to irk everyone with his remarks—even the conservatives he claimed to be speaking for.

He was the next Never Kevin and began courting alternative Speaker candidates as early as the summer of 2022, reportedly approaching several other members of our conference he viewed as better suited to his brand of conservatism and signaling that these individuals could count on his support were they to throw their hat in the ring.

The third Never Kevin was an individual we did not initially foresee falling into this camp, former Freedom Caucus Chair Andy Biggs of Arizona. He made his position known via an op-ed released on November 18 that stated: "[I] cannot and will not vote for Kevin for Speaker."

In the moment, reading those words was a total gut punch. It caught all of us by surprise and rattled our cages. Worse still, this public statement left Biggs no wiggle room or ambiguity and meant we could only afford to lose one more member before our path was blocked entirely.

Biggs's tenure as Freedom Caucus Chair was mostly served in the minority, but it included some moments when Kevin and the group worked hand in glove, particularly on fighting back against the first impeachment of President Trump. But Biggs never really found his footing as chair and failed to unify the group in the way that Mark Meadows or Jim Jordan had.

On the few occasions when I did inquire about the root of his opposition, Biggs's only response to me was, "Kevin knows why I'm a no." Yet for the life of us, neither Kevin nor I could ever figure out what he meant besides perhaps feeling that we had not kept him in the loop and spent enough time with him when he was leading the HFC.

Biggs also openly floated the idea of a "consensus candidate" to supersede Kevin.

"I can think of probably twenty people who nobody's mad at ever," he told the press, going so far as to single out a more junior member of our leadership table, Louisiana Representative Mike Johnson, who served as Vice Chair of the Conference. Johnson was one of the individuals whom Bob Good had approached, as well.

"I don't think people get mad at him too often," Biggs said of Johnson, who was best known at that time for organizing various competitions that incentivized members to stay on message with prizes like miniature busts of Patrick Henry and John Adams.

Next up in this group was Matt Rosendale of Montana, our friend who previously admitted he was rooting against Republicans in the midterm elections. While he didn't outright say he was a hard no, his demeanor and public comments certainly didn't seem positive.

"I refuse to elect the same people utilizing the same rules that keep us from—members like me—from participating," Rosendale told former Trump adviser Steve Bannon on Bannon's *War Room* podcast that November.

Rosendale was a former state Senate president in Montana, and we originally thought he might be someone who would understand the competing pressures that leaders of legislative bodies needed to juggle. Unfortunately, we quickly realized that would not be the case.

Apparently, in Rosendale's Montana state Senate, nearly every bill filed by a member received floor consideration, and members were often allowed to offer unlimited amendments. While that might have worked in a small statehouse that only convened for a few weeks at a time, the US House of Representatives saw over 10,000 bills filed each Congress. If we used those same procedures, the House would barely make it through a few dozen bills each Congress—and none of them would likely pass after the parade of nonstop "gotcha" amendments.

After shouting at Kevin about his views on how the House should run, spittle flying from his mouth, Rosendale added his second main issue: reinstating the one-person Motion to Vacate, a term I will describe in greater detail in a later chapter and that you will become all too familiar with by the end of this book.

"That is nonnegotiable. Simply nonnegotiable," Rosendale asserted about the Motion to Vacate.

"I don't think the conference will go for that," Kevin calmly replied.

"Well, then see you in January!" he screamed.

With that, the meeting was over. Another vote lost for a total of four between Gaetz, Good, Biggs, and Rosendale. Any more defections, and we would be below the 218 threshold needed to win.

Camp 2: Maybe Kevins

While the Never Kevins did their best to kick up dirt, the second camp was one we understood to be skeptical, but not yet closed off, otherwise known as the Maybe Kevins.

Unlike the former group, who simply wanted to block Kevin out of spite, this group of about fifteen or so members from the Freedom Caucus viewed their opposition to Kevin as a means to enhance their own clout inside Congress through new rules and procedures that were more favorable to them. Think better committee assignments, greater say in what bills came to the floor and with what amendments, and other guardrails to prevent the leadership from circumventing their small yet vocal contingent.

This was the group where I devoted the majority of my time and effort, telling Kevin over the summer that I would make it my personal mission to ensure that Chip Roy of Texas, the unofficial leader of the Maybe Kevins, voted for him for Speaker.

"I'm not sure. I don't know if he ever gets there," Kevin replied when I told him of my plan.

"Give me some time," I said.

Although Chip was not the elected chairman of the Freedom Caucus, it seemed clear to me that he was the true center of gravity of the group. And I believed that if we could get Chip to commit to Kevin, the others would eventually fall in line too.

A former chief of staff to Texas Senator Ted Cruz, Chip generally understood the mechanics of governing, as well as the role staff played in the process. That might explain why he got to know so many of us floor staff—a basic step that I was frankly shocked more members didn't take the time to do.

He and I would text on a regular basis, largely discussing floor tactics and strategy, but also interspersing in random tweets about sports or music. Chip was fond of the Twitter account @Super70sSports, which I thankfully knew just enough about to be dangerous.

Unlike some of the newer Freedom Caucus members, Chip was not a blind acolyte of Donald Trump—arguing loudly, for example, against Trump's push for Congress to object to certification of the 2020 presidential election.

This extended to his priorities for the upcoming Congress, as well. He cast doubt on the growing focus on investigating Hunter Biden and said he would even be open to raising taxes in a Grand Bargain–style deal to address the national debt.

"Fuck Grover," he told me, referring to Grover Norquist, president of Americans for Tax Reform and architect of the pledge that aspiring Republican lawmakers would sign to oppose any and all tax increases.

Above all, I felt that Chip was someone we could work with, and I think he felt the same. My wife often joked that in the fall of 2022, there were actually three occupants in our tiny Navy Yard apartment—her, myself, and Chip Roy calling my cell phone. Later, I was told by his staffers that they also had a similar joke in the office—a constant stream from Chip each morning of "Leganski said this" or "Leganski said that."

Chip and I held several marathon meetings in his DC office that fall—part strategy discussions, part therapy sessions. His default posture was "Let's get in a room, let's roll up our sleeves, and let's hash this out—no matter how long it takes."

While some of Chip's advice was helpful, much of it was also self-contradicting—something even he acknowledged.

On the one hand, he said his group wanted a Speaker who was inspiring, someone who would rally the members and lay out a clear, step-by-step plan of action.

"We need a real plan," he told me. "Not just words."

On the other hand, his group also claimed to want the Speaker to be less hands-on and to decentralize decision-making, having felt burned by the past three Speakers calling the shots from on high.

In addition, the group wanted a Speaker to channel the anger and sense of urgency they felt about the issues, someone who knew "what time it was." But when pressed for specifics, Chip would reply simply: "You know it when you see it."

"We need transformational change," he would repeat.

After hearing this for the umpteenth time, I felt compelled to respond.

"That paradigm shift is already here," I explained, pointing to the slim five-seat majority we held going into the 118th Congress that would allow

Chip and any four of his friends to grind business to a halt. "We need to front-load all of our work so we identify problems at the start and don't blow ourselves up on the launching pad," I argued.

"What I'll say is this: No one currently has 218," he replied.

"I hear you. But someone eventually *does* need to get to 218," I said. "It's not enough to just block 218. We also need to be able to build 218—week in and week out this entire Congress."

While the Freedom Caucus was excellent at reflexively voting no, building a majority coalition of yes votes never happened to be their strong suit.

* * *

At the conclusion of that particular meeting, Chip's team called me to say that they thought our conversation went as well as could be hoped for. Moreover, they reiterated their view that Chip would vote for Kevin if he felt the HFC got a deal that was too good to walk away from.

My approach to the holdouts was largely shaped by a lengthy phone conversation I was fortunate enough to have early in my career with Andy Card, former White House chief of staff for President George W. Bush.

When I asked Card for his advice on dealing with a frustrating group of seemingly intractable members, he offered two thoughts.

"Well, John, they were elected," he said, "They have a right to be there."

Simple as that message was, it was a good personal reminder that voters sent those members to Washington to represent them. We had to work with them—whether we liked it or not.

To punctuate his point, Card told an anecdote about a movie night President Bush held at the White House the evening after a particularly hard-fought vote. Card was aghast that a senator who voted against the White House's position that day was still invited to the event, smiling and enjoying the perks of an exclusive evening at 1600 Pennsylvania Avenue.

Card angrily asked the President if he wanted the senator to be removed.

"We didn't get him today, Andy," Bush calmly said. "But we might need him tomorrow."

As it did for Card, that observation left a lasting impression upon me.

Even so, I knew better than to fully trust what Chip or any of the other Freedom Caucus members were relaying.

That fall, for instance, we discovered a so-called McCarthy Dossier that Chip had in his possession and left behind on the House floor, of all places. It was almost so obvious that I wasn't sure whether or not it was left there with the intention of being found.

The document itself was pretty underwhelming, largely a series of supposedly "bad votes" that Kevin had taken over the years, mostly votes for government funding bills or debt ceiling increases. The most useful tidbit for us was the full roster of the Freedom Caucus—a list they famously kept closely guarded like the Coca-Cola secret formula—including what committees they served on and what subcommittee gavels they held. To be safe, we made a copy and left it back where we found it.

Through it all, I continued to remind myself and our team that this race would be a marathon, not a sprint. Back in 2015, Kevin's run for Speaker started and ended in less than fifteen days but felt like an eternity when we were in the eye of the storm. This time around, we would need to endure over two months until the floor vote, holding the Gaetz crew of Never Kevins at bay while simultaneously winning over the Chip Roys and the Maybe Kevins of the world.

Trouble ahead, trouble behind. What could possibly go wrong?

CHAPTER 9

SECRET BALLOTS

Before the official January swearing-in, each Congress would hold "new member orientation," a multi-week affair that saw members-elect descend on Washington for a string of events aimed to prepare them for their new life as a representative.

On the Democratic side, a major shake-up was underway, with Speaker Nancy Pelosi announcing that she would not seek another term in House leadership after twenty years leading the caucus.

"The hour has come for a new generation to lead the Democratic caucus that I so deeply respect," she stated in her final floor speech as Speaker.

Democratic Majority Leader Steny Hoyer of Maryland released a similar statement shortly thereafter saying that he would also forgo running for an elected leadership position. From my vantage point on the floor, however, he looked downright pissed as he listened to Pelosi close the door on him ever serving as Speaker, another victim of the Curse of the Majority Leader.

That said, aside from Steny, it was downright giddy on the Democratic side of the aisle. Pelosi's departure paved the way for Hakeem Jeffries of New York to ascend to minority leader, Katherine Clark of Massachusetts to rise to minority whip, and Pete Aguilar of California to be elected caucus chair—our new counterparts in leadership. All three of their promotions were unanimous, with dozens and dozens of members from all corners of their party tripping over each other to give nominating speeches, each more glowing than the last.

Democrats had lost the House majority—they should have been miserable. But like the Whos down in Whoville on Christmas morning, the Grinch hadn't stolen their joy. Instead, they greatly outperformed expectations in the 2022 midterms and felt as though they had wind behind their sails heading into the 2024 cycle, similar to how we felt in 2020. Now, they were able to toast the leadership triumvirate that had led them for decades—Pelosi, Hoyer, and Democratic Assistant Speaker Jim Clyburn of South Carolina—while seamlessly welcoming in a fresh trio of new faces. They might as well have been singing "Kumbaya."

Our Republican organizing meetings would be nothing of the sort.

* * *

First on the docket was the candidate forum, where any and all candidates for leadership positions were invited to give brief opening statements before fielding questions from members of the conference. Typically, these were somewhat sleepy, low-drama affairs. But attendance at this particular meeting on Monday, November 14 was as high as I had ever seen it.

The order went from Speaker on down, putting Kevin on stage first. While the Freedom Caucus threatened to run a candidate of their own for Speaker if we did not accede to their demands to delay the upcoming party elections, we figured they would probably run someone against us either way and chose to barrel ahead instead.

After Kevin delivered his brief opening statement, Matt Gaetz of Florida made a beeline to the microphones set up at the front of the auditorium for the question-and-answer session.

"Have you ever or would you ever solicit votes from Democrats for Speaker?" Gaetz queried, a pointed reference to a news report from earlier in the week that alleged certain Republicans were in talks with moderate Texas Democrat Henry Cuellar about what it might take to win his vote for Speaker.

"No, never have and never will," Kevin replied curtly.

From where I sat, this was a classic Gaetz tactic: "Heads, I win—tails, you lose."

If Kevin and our allies were courting Democrats, Gaetz could have tried to paint us in the press as a squish, choosing to work with Democrats before Republicans even took the majority.

Conversely, if moderate Democrats like Cuellar were not on the table, then Gaetz would continue to hold a significant amount of leverage by virtue of using his Never Kevin crew as a blocking mechanism. And based on the satisfied grin on his face after hearing Kevin's response, the latter seemed to be Gaetz's preference.

* * *

After Kevin's queue ended, the mic was handed off to the candidate running unopposed for the position of majority leader, Louisiana Representative Steve Scalise.

An entire chapter could probably be dedicated to the relationship between Kevin and Steve, but I will give you the condensed version here.

As mentioned in chapter 1, the two originally met as Young Republicans before going on to serve in their respective statehouses in California and Louisiana. While Kevin was elected to the House in 2006, Steve followed two years later, winning a special election in 2008 to fill the congressional seat previously held by future Louisiana Governor Bobby Jindal.

From there, it was a swift ascent up the leadership ladder for both, with Kevin moving from chief deputy whip to majority whip to majority leader in just six years—the fastest such rise in history—while Steve parlayed his chairmanship of the Republican Study Committee into a victory in the open contest for majority whip two years later.

Perhaps it was simply natural for a rivalry to develop between ambitious lawmakers, particularly those who were one rung apart from one another and could judge the person now doing the job they once did. After all, look no further than Nancy Pelosi and Steny Hoyer or Barack Obama and Joe Biden.

In general, however, Steve's first few years as whip were fairly unremarkable, the most noteworthy moment of which surrounded a 2014 controversy over the unearthing of a speech he delivered in 2002 to a white nationalist group with ties to Ku Klux Klan grand wizard David Duke that threatened to drive him from Congress entirely.

That all changed dramatically in 2017 when a shooting at the practice of the Republican congressional baseball team critically wounded Steve and injured four others. Steve's recovery was nothing short of a miracle, and his triumphant return to the House Chamber was one of the more emotional scenes I ever witnessed on the floor.

"You have no idea how great this feels to be back at work at the People's House," he said to several loud ovations. "I'm a living example that miracles really do happen."

Steve's bravery in the face of tragedy rightfully catapulted him into near-mythical status inside the famously rough-and-tumble House, with President Trump dubbing him "the Legend from Louisiana" during his State of the Union address the following year.

It was against this backdrop that the relationship entered a more complex phase, with Steve mulling a challenge to Kevin in 2018 for the top job after Speaker Ryan departed from the House. While that head-to-head showdown never materialized despite Kevin personally daring Steve to do so, the on-and-off tension between the two men and their respective teams persisted, with our camp consistently hearing rumors of Steve and his allies making preparations behind the scenes for us to fail and sowing doubt in Washington about Kevin's ability to secure 218 votes.

By the time 2022 rolled around, multiple outlets were pointing to Steve as a potential alternative to Kevin, including an *Axios* piece that quoted several unnamed members who referred to him as "the great compromise" candidate.

Unsurprisingly, Gaetz sought to stir the pot, as well.

"No one ran against [Steve Scalise] for Majority Leader. He was elected unanimously for that position," Gaetz told *The New York Post* that November, an implicit suggestion that Scalise theoretically possessed a path to 218 votes on paper.

Our suspicions were only heightened when Gaetz returned to the microphone to ask Steve a question at the candidate forum. Specifically, Gaetz asked if Steve would like to apologize for comments revealed in a leaked audio recording taken after January 6, 2021, in which he suggested that Gaetz's inflammatory social media posts were potentially worthy of an investigation or him going to jail.

"Yes, I would like to apologize," Steve told Matt. "I didn't have all the facts when I was speaking at that time and was just going off of what I had heard."

To most members in the room, the question probably felt out of left field. But to keen observers, it served as a way for Gaetz to publicly clear the air with Steve, potentially teeing him up as Gaetz's preferred alternative for Speaker.

"Our relationship is on the ascent," Gaetz told the press of Scalise later that month.

* * *

The most heated internal contest that year was for the number three position of majority whip among Tom Emmer of Minnesota, Drew Ferguson of Georgia, and Jim Banks of Indiana. The race was not without consequence, as I felt that whoever won would eventually be the person best positioned to succeed Kevin down the road given the whip's natural proximity to the broader membership.

As the chair of the House Republicans' campaign apparatus, Tom Emmer seemed to have the clear edge heading into the midterms. A hockey fanatic and father of seven, Emmer had quickly climbed the House leadership ladder, himself—showing a knack for both bare-knuckled electoral politics and interpersonal member management, two skills that were essential for any aspiring whip.

However, the underwhelming election results cut against him in two ways. First, it sapped him of dozens of potential new freshmen members he had likely been counting on to vote for him, individuals with whom he had become close during the campaign process who would have been inclined to repay the favor.

Second, like after any disappointing sports season, the rhetorical calls to find a scapegoat and "make a change at the top" began to grow louder, with the other candidates arguing that simply giving each of the elected leaders a blanket promotion was a bad way to ensure accountability—particularly for the person whose job was to oversee our conference's campaign efforts.

Drew Ferguson was the next candidate, most well-known for being Steve Scalise's top lieutenant during both terms in the minority as chief deputy whip. The two southerners had become close allies over the years, even utilizing shared staff between their offices. Not surprisingly, Steve whipped hard for Drew in both public and private, and Drew's candidacy eventually became another proxy battle of sorts in the ongoing cold war between the McCarthy and Scalise camps.

The final candidate was Jim Banks, a former chair of the Republican Study Committee who ran as the insurgent, upstart candidate. A future senator from Indiana, Banks was personally close with Kevin and had previously been tapped to serve as ranking member of the January 6th Select Committee before Speaker Pelosi made the unprecedented decision to block both his and Jim Jordan's appointments to the panel.

Internally, our team was divided between Banks and Emmer, with our chief of staff, Dan Meyer, tending to favor his fellow Minnesotan Emmer, while our deputy chief of staff, James Min, had developed a closer relationship with Banks's team.

On the one hand, elevating Banks could quell some of the conservative concerns about the makeup of the leadership table and quiet the "everyone shouldn't get a promotion" narrative. On the other, Emmer had been a loyal soldier throughout, and his team and ours had developed an excellent working relationship over the years in our quest to take back the majority.

While Kevin officially remained neutral in the contest, he certainly did not encourage anyone to vote for Ferguson.

* * *

The internal party elections to decide each of the above races occurred the following day, Tuesday, November 15.

Late Monday evening, the press reported that former chair of the Freedom Caucus, Arizona Representative Andy Biggs, would put his name forward to be the Republican nominee for Speaker of the House. My friend Chip Roy gave Biggs's official nomination speech, with Michael Cloud of Texas and Ralph Norman of South Carolina seconding Biggs's nomination.

As for us, Kevin chose Kelly Armstrong of North Dakota, Kat Cammack of Florida, and Brian Fitzpatrick of Pennsylvania to deliver his nominating speeches, with the moderate Fitzpatrick concluding his remarks by laying down a clear marker of his own to the detractors.

"That's why I will be voting for Kevin and *only* Kevin for Speaker of the House," he said to applause.

That statement unofficially kickstarted the creation of a third camp: the Only Kevins. After all, just as any group of five could block Kevin's path to 218 votes on the floor, so too could any other determined group of five block a different candidate's path.

"I don't care if it's the first vote or the fiftieth vote. I'm voting for McCarthy," future governor Kelly Armstrong later echoed to the press. "Anyone else who gets to 218 does it without me. North Dakota is closed for winter right now anyway. I have nowhere to be."

In other words: We can play that game too.

* * *

At the conclusion of all nominating speeches, it was time for balloting. Each member would come forward to claim a secret ballot roughly the size of a third of a sheet of paper. The ballots were indistinguishable from one another, denoting the position at the top the members would be voting for—"Speaker of the House"—and then providing a blank line underneath to write the name of their preferred candidate.

This was the congressional version of electing a Pope, though the Capitol Visitors Center auditorium certainly bore no comparison to the Sistine Chapel. Even so, the process itself was almost equally as slow, with time seeming to inch to a crawl for us staff.

We knew Kevin would easily prevail in the vote. The question on everyone's mind was: *By how much?*

After nearly forty-five minutes of balloting and tabulation, Chairwoman Elise Stefanik of New York banged the gavel to declare the outcome.

"The Chair is prepared to announce the result of the election for Speaker," she began.

"The tellers agree in their tallies: Mr. McCarthy received 188 votes, Mr. Biggs received 31 votes. The Chair announces that the Honorable Kevin McCarthy, having received a majority of the votes cast, a quorum being present, is therefore duly elected Speaker-designee for the 118th Congress. The

Chair now recognizes the next Speaker of the House," she declared, the room rising to an ovation.

One hundred and eighty-eight votes was a strong showing, and we were quite pleased with the tally, which tracked closely with our internal whip count. By way of comparison, Paul Ryan lost forty-three votes to Daniel Webster of Florida in 2015 during the same internal conference balloting. Likewise, Nancy Pelosi had thirty-two defections in her 2018 Democratic caucus elections. So Kevin's thirty-one defections did not look terribly insurmountable on paper.

What the chair did not announce, however, but what certain sources made sure to alert the press of afterward was that there were also five individuals who voted for other candidates beyond McCarthy or Biggs that were not reflected in this publicly announced tally.

While those votes were never made public since they were not votes for officially nominated candidates, we were informed that these stray votes included one vote for Steve Scalise, one for Jim Jordan, one for Mike Johnson of Louisiana, one for former representative Lee Zeldin of New York, and one who wrote down "present."

Whether intentional or not, we viewed these five "others" as a purposeful sign that even if Kevin convinced all thirty-one of Biggs's supporters to vote for him, there was still a bloc of five prepared to deny us on the floor, a fact that Matt Gaetz was all too eager to reiterate in the press.

"He couldn't get the votes in six years, and he's not going to get the votes in the next six weeks," Gaetz told the media that day.

More worrisome, CNN quoted an anonymous GOP lawmaker who stated: "The strategy is to drip out a name every four or five days, or every week, just to make sure people know."

"It's not just four or five," the lawmaker added.

Underneath the bravado and well-rehearsed lines, though, we sensed more than a little fear in Gaetz and the Never Kevins, with close ally Patrick McHenry of North Carolina confronting Gaetz after the meeting to push for answers on his endgame.

"You know Kevin's never going to quit—right, Matt?" McHenry asked the Floridian.

"No, that's not how I want this to go," Gaetz replied, insisting that Kevin needed to see the writing on the wall and drop out before the January floor election as he had in 2015.

"Matt, I know that's not what you want. But that's what Kevin is going to do," McHenry stated. "He is never dropping out."

"No! That's not how I want this to go!" Gaetz whined louder this time, storming off in frustration.

* * *

Following our race and Steve Scalise's unopposed election as majority leader, the whip race delivered the real drama for the day.

Team Emmer had signaled confidence for the better part of the past month, with Banks's campaign claiming that it was picking up steam. Ferguson was the real wild card, but I did not sense a ton of confidence coming from their corner as the vote neared.

The first round of balloting came back as close as could be: Banks in the lead with 82, Emmer in second with 72, Ferguson in last with 71. One vote was all that separated the second- and third-place finishers.

For the first time all week, the room audibly gasped.

I happened to be standing near Emmer when the vote total was announced and he cursed aloud to himself, "Shit!"

Our conference rules dictated that if no candidate received an outright majority, the lowest vote-getter would drop off the ballot—in this case, Ferguson—and the members would then proceed to another round of voting among the remaining candidates.

There were only a few minutes before the second round of balloting began, with Banks's team furiously whipping known Ferguson supporters to see if they could persuade them to throw their support to Banks. Likewise for Emmer, though his operation seemed to handle the outreach more via text, with Guy Reschenthaler of Pennsylvania taking a lead role in working the room.

In the end, the more tenured "old bull" supporters of Ferguson broke for Emmer by a count of 43–24, preferring to stick with the guy they knew and enabling Emmer to prevail 115–106 over Banks. Had that first round gone differently, however, Drew Ferguson very well could have taken a similar percentage breakdown of Emmer's votes to emerge victorious. In fact, a member later confided to a reporter on background that they mistakenly wrote down Emmer when they intended to write down Ferguson during round one—a move that would have eliminated Emmer on the first ballot and potentially changed the course of history in the House.

Further down the line, Elise Stefanik of New York lost seventy-four votes but managed to defeat rising Florida representative and regular Fox News presence Byron Donalds for the position of conference chair—the Freedom Caucus' most concerted attempt to date to elect one of their own to leadership. Meanwhile, Mike Johnson of Louisiana ran unopposed for a second term as conference vice chair—the seventh-ranking position in the hierarchy—to round out our leadership table for the 118th Congress.

CHAPTER 10

THE FIVE FAMILIES

The third day of organizing meetings was dedicated to considering amendments to the Republican conference rules, a document less than twenty pages long that was used to govern our internal meetings and processes, not much different than what you would use to run your typical homeowners' association.

But just as every community has that one annoying neighbor who tries to use such rules to ruin everything, the Freedom Caucus had begun to weaponize these rules in recent years to force party members to take votes on various nonbinding resolutions or "positions," similar to how they ran their HFC meetings. That meant we needed to take each amendment seriously and defeat the more destructive ones.

For reference, only nine potential amendments were submitted for consideration in the prior Congress, the large majority of which were noncontroversial. In 2022, we saw three times as many for a total of twenty-seven, almost entirely from the Freedom Caucus.

While Kevin strongly supported the rights of members to have a say in the legislative process and do what they thought was necessary to best represent their constituents, it was not clear that the Freedom Caucus' proposals were aimed at achieving such noble ends so much so as they were designed to get the proverbial "camel's nose under the tent" and empower themselves to cause further gridlock.

Even if viewed in the most generous of lights, their proposals more often seemed to be solutions in search of a problem that proved self-contradictory.

For example, one of their top priorities was an amendment to formalize the "Hastert Rule"—named for the operating principle used by the disgraced former Speaker—which stated that a bill could only come to the floor if we could verify before the vote that it had the support of a "majority of the majority." In theory, this would ensure that any bills that passed the Republican-led House would be sufficiently conservative.

But while this "majority of the majority" benchmark was held up as the gold standard, for some reason it was not good enough that Kevin had just demonstrated that he possessed the support of a supermajority of the conference. Instead, the Freedom Caucus was still threatening to vote against him on the floor, holding the majority of the majority captive to a small minority.

In an effort to keep the process more manageable, we split the amendments into two batches and reserved time for an additional meeting after the Thanksgiving holiday. We stacked the handful of noncontroversial ideas in the first tranche alongside the more egregious ideas where we saw no middle ground for compromise, and we saved the ideas on which there was a potential for negotiations and modifications for the later session.

Although we accepted numerous amendments from Freedom Caucus members that day—including ideas from Lauren Boebert of Colorado, Andrew Clyde of Georgia, and Gary Palmer of Alabama—we soundly defeated some of their more irrational proposals that would have severely undermined our ability to govern. Needless to say, the Freedom Caucus did not respond favorably to our efforts.

"It was clear that the conference leadership had lined up opposition to go to the mic to talk against every rule proposal, every change that we put forward, or just about every one," Bob Good of Virginia told the press after the meeting.

"I was disappointed about how the rules meeting was conducted," Freedom Caucus Chair Scott Perry added. "Unless something changes, they should get used to that, because the tenor of that meeting was exactly what I've experienced throughout my time in Congress."

"There's a whole hell of a lot of work to do for someone who gets to 218," Chip Roy concluded.

* * *

While the day was a victory for keeping our conference rules intact, the brewing discontent inside the Freedom Caucus was palpable and threatened to snowball into more public defections from Kevin as Congress departed for the Thanksgiving recess.

Hoping to head off such a backlash, I drafted up another "Dear Colleague" letter that weekend to reset the narrative, calm the waters, and buy us some time. We remained open to working with the Freedom Caucus—after all, there was no path to 218 without them. But there needed to be some give-and-take so any changes to our rules actually made sense.

Kevin recommended that we run the draft letter by a few other members to serve as an informal focus group. For me, Patrick McHenry of North Carolina was one of my reliable go-to members for such a job.

A bow tie–wearing North Carolinian, McHenry was first elected to Congress in 2005 at just twenty-nine years old. Young and brash, he began his legislative career as a bomb-thrower, not that dissimilar in temperament and style from the group of members we were now trying to win over. But in time, he learned to deftly play the inside game, serving for five years as Steve Scalise's chief deputy whip before being tapped to lead the House Financial Services committee. Through it all, he kept his finger on the pulse of the conference as well as anyone and remained a loyal Kevin confidant.

"What is the point of this letter?" McHenry pressed me.

"We need to stop the bleeding," I said. "Stem the tide of public nos and show that we're willing to change the way we operate."

After walking through my thinking and where we stood with the large group of undecideds, McHenry concurred with the approach and summarized what would become our overarching strategy moving forward: Hold the two hundred supporters we had, while breaking the twenty holdouts.

Hold the two hundred, break the twenty, I repeated in my head.

"We need to give Kevin the best shot to win them over as only he can, one-on-one," Patrick said. "There is no one better in that setting than him."

* * *

Later that day, Kevin sent the final version of the letter to our conference.

"I want to thank everyone who actively participated and who is offering up concrete ideas for how we make this place run better," he began. "For my part, I am committed to changing the way we do business—both as a conference and as a Congress—to include more voices at the table, ensure all viewpoints are represented on committees, give Members greater say in the legislative process, and decentralize decision-making."

"Not everyone will get everything they want," he concluded, "But I am open to working with all Members on ways to empower our conference and advance conservative principles, while not ceding control of the Floor to Democrats."

Kevin also announced an upcoming trip that he would be taking to the US-Mexico border over the holiday, with border security continuing to be one of the top issues in America and one of the most unifying issues inside our conference. While there, he served turkey dinners to our border patrol and ICE agents in El Paso, Texas, and previewed a series of aggressive actions that our majority would take to address the flow of migrants streaming across, including a potential impeachment inquiry into Department of Homeland Security Secretary Alejandro Mayorkas.

In general, the letter was well received and appeared to serve its intended purpose. Virginia Representative Ben Cline, a rare member of both the ultra-conservative Freedom Caucus and the bipartisan Problem Solvers Caucus, texted our team to say it was "pitch perfect" and that he would be encouraging his fellow conservatives to keep their powder dry and work with us.

At the same time, I set up a meeting with Tim Reitz, the lead staffer for the Freedom Caucus, to begin hashing out edits to their remaining proposals.

Tim had a tough job as one of the only full-time staffers employed by the Freedom Caucus. But we always seemed to get along well, both socially and professionally. At the end of the day, most of us staffers were just trying to do right by our bosses and get home at a reasonable hour.

"Look, my guys were pretty upset with the way things went down last week," Tim told me during a meeting in our office that following Monday.

"I understand. But you know a lot of those ideas just weren't going to fly," I replied. "Let's try to see if we can find some common ground on the rest."

We pored through their remaining proposals, one by one, for almost two hours. "Blue pens" was my mantra—as in, how do we add, edit, build upon, create—versus "red pens," which were simply used for saying no and crossing things out. It was a riff on one of Kevin's lines that he would use when he felt like our staff was only shooting down ideas: "Easy with the red pens, guys."

Unfortunately, only a few hours after Tim and I concluded, my phone buzzed with over a dozen texts from friends linking to a story where yet another Freedom Caucus member had announced that he was no longer going to support Kevin for Speaker: South Carolina Representative Ralph Norman.

* * *

"Washington is broken," the South Carolina conservative told *Just the News*. "There's a cancer in this country and it can't be fixed with aspirin. It's called overspending."

Norman's opposition came totally out of left field for us, particularly after Kevin had gone to bat for him inside the Steering Committee that June and elevated him to serve on the powerful House Financial Services Committee.

For me, it re-created that same feeling of the wind being knocked out of you that I experienced when Andy Biggs went public with his no. More concerning, Norman was now the critical fifth public no, enough to deny us the votes necessary to win on the floor.

I texted the story to a friend who used to work for Norman: "WTF?"

"That'll be a surprise to his staff," he replied.

"Can you figure out what the deal is?" I asked.

"Yeah, just asked his chief, who confirmed he was blindsided."

"Is there wiggle room?" I asked.

"Strikes me as a 'caught up in the moment' thing—but I really don't know and neither does his staff at the moment," my friend replied.

Any hopes for a backtracking were dashed when Norman went on Steve Bannon's podcast a few days later to restate his opposition.

Kevin sent a one-word response to our group chain—"unbelievable"—and then called me to suggest that he simply go scorched earth on the Freedom Caucus. I channeled that anger in a screaming match with Tim Reitz, myself.

"Why are we even putting in this work?" I yelled at Tim. "We'll just beat the remainder of your ideas and save ourselves the time!"

We went a few rounds like this back and forth, but we eventually calmed down and agreed to reconvene after the holiday. If nothing else, I think the message was received that we were not happy—and the Freedom Caucus' previously rumored drip-drop strategy of slowly growing the list of public nos failed to materialize.

* * *

That Thanksgiving, I was able to enjoy a rare day off work as Giulia and I spent the holiday with some close friends and their family in Arlington, Virginia. The following day, our chief of staff, Dan Meyer, our communications director, Matt Sparks, and I were even able to sneak in a round of golf at Mount Vernon Country Club.

We managed to avoid the elephant in the room for the first few holes, but eventually one of us asked the other the question on everyone's minds: *What if this doesn't work out?*

Matt—or "Sparks," as we called him—suggested that his career could very well be done on the Hill, with Kevin having been his first and only boss in Washington. He first joined the office in 2012 when I was an intern and worked his way up from unpaid staffer to one of Kevin's most trusted senior advisers, in addition to becoming one of my best friends.

In many ways, Sparks was singlehandedly responsible for the dramatic inroads we had made with the right-wing ecosystem over the past seven years, a group that was now pummeling the public nos—or "the Five Saboteurs" as conservative commentator Mark Levin had branded them—on Twitter and on television on a daily basis.

Regardless of our musings, it was simply cathartic to speak freely for a few moments about that which no one had previously dared to contemplate out loud. But while it was liberating to mentally escape for a minute and imagine a world away from the mess that we now found ourselves in, we both agreed that we had come too far to turn back now.

"We should do whatever it takes to win," I told him at our post-round lunch at Mike's American, a classic two-story eatery in Springfield, Virginia. "That's how I really feel."

"I agree," Sparks replied. "It's now or never."

We spitballed other ideas that could help pry things loose, such as naming Jim Jordan of Ohio to be Assistant Speaker, a similar tactic to what Pelosi did in elevating Jim Clyburn of South Carolina to be her Assistant Speaker.

"Failure is not an option," we agreed.

We also brainstormed how to make the most out of a pivotal upcoming meeting our team had arranged with select members of the Freedom Caucus and a larger cross section of the conference. In particular, Sparks and I wanted to find something to break the ice off the bat so that members would be able to settle in a little bit.

In the end, we settled on a quote from Don Corleone in *The Godfather* during the famous scene of the meeting of the Five Families.

"I hoped that we could come here and reason together. And as a reasonable man, I'm willing to do whatever's necessary to find a peaceful solution to these problems."

* * *

The meeting was set for the Tuesday after Thanksgiving in our office, with the goal being to get members back together in a room, engaged, and talking with one another about the path forward. Internally, we were mindful of a piece of advice relayed by Freedom Caucus member Dave Schweikert of Arizona.

"You have to remember that these kids were the nerds in high school," Schweikert told us. "They want to know that you're not going to go back to shoving them in the locker when you become captain of the football team. They want to be able to sit at the cool kids' table."

Kevin was a little unsure when we first reviewed the slides and showed him the quote from Don Corleone, but it thankfully had the intended effect in the meeting. While you could just about cut the tension with a knife as members began to take their seats, nearly everyone in the room laughed when

Kevin flipped to the first slide and explained how we also had "Five Families" represented around the table.

There was the Republican Study Committee or RSC, the largest and oldest conservative bloc in the House, chaired by Kevin Hern of Oklahoma.

The Republican Governance Group, formerly known as "The Tuesday Group," a more moderate collection of predominantly midwestern and northeastern members, chaired by Dave Joyce of Ohio.

The Main Street Caucus, a business-minded centrist group chaired by Don Bacon of Nebraska.

The Problem Solvers Caucus, a bipartisan group that regularly met with compromise-minded Democrats, chaired by Brian Fitzpatrick of Pennsylvania.

And of course, the archconservative House Freedom Caucus, chaired by Scott Perry of Pennsylvania.

"As you know if you've seen the movie," Kevin reminded the group, "if we don't find a peaceful solution to these problems, we all end up killing each other."

After a hearty, perhaps too-on-the-nose laugh, the meeting proceeded in a fairly productive manner, with dozens of members from all Five Families having a healthy and vigorous debate about both our conference rules and the rules for the House floor.

"This is how we are going to have to do things from now on," Kevin explained. "The margin is such that everyone has veto power over everyone else. But if we can front-load our challenges and work them out before we go to the floor, we will be more successful."

That tenor carried over into our final conference-wide organizing meeting, as well, with Tim Reitz and I pulling a near all-nighter the evening prior, trading edits back and forth right up until the meeting began. In the end, we found common ground on a variety of their amendments, including a Scott Perry proposal to require a party meeting before consideration of major pieces of legislation, a Dan Bishop proposal to more quickly debate and vote on internal party positions within the House Republican Conference, and two proposals from Chip Roy, one that would require more advance notice on certain fast-tracked bills and another that made it easier for rank-and-file amendments to be made in order on the floor.

Despite some minor grumblings from the center of the conference, we walked out happy with the results. Both sides felt like they got something, but neither got everything. Equally as important, Kevin received a lot of kudos for how he handled the meeting from the group of twenty we were trying to win over.

"It was much more amicable today, as it should be," Scott Perry said.

Perhaps we were turning a corner. The Freedom Caucus had finally been invited to the cool kids' table, and maybe—just maybe—we were figuring out how to build some level of trust and find a way to make this chaotic majority work.

CHAPTER 11

TERMS OF SURRENDER

While we were intentional about using a carrot approach on the inside, the Freedom Caucus had also been subjected to an increasing dose of sticks from our friends and allies on the outside. Specifically, we found that the most effective line of attack that resonated with our base was pointing out that the Freedom Caucus' antics could result in the election of a more moderate member as Speaker.

Maven reporter Matthew Boyle detailed such a doomsday scenario in a buzzy story on the conservative website Breitbart with citations to numerous state legislatures that saw members of the minority join together with a handful of members in the majority to install a more centrist candidate in the top job, including Arkansas in 2012, Pennsylvania in 2007, and New Jersey in 1971, to name a few.

Shortly thereafter, Georgia Representative Marjorie Taylor Greene tweeted a link to the story, stating "I refuse to allow the Uniparty to choose the Speaker of the House and lose our opportunity to subpoena, investigate, and block the Democrats' America Last agenda. Our GOP Conference must unite behind Speaker-elect Kevin McCarthy."

Centrist Representative Don Bacon of Nebraska added further fuel to the fire by telling the press that he would be open to working with Democrats to elect a "unity Speaker" rather than simply rolling over to whatever and whoever the hard right demanded.

"If these five or six will not play ball at all, then I will work across the aisle with Democrats," Bacon told the press—with our blessing, of course.

That was followed by Progressive Democrat Ro Khanna of California issuing a similar statement that he, too, would be open to voting for a moderate Republican Speaker under the right conditions, such as a more equitable power-sharing agreement for his party, giving even further credence to the idea.

While Hill staff were no stranger to the Freedom Caucus' tendency to score own goals, this series of events sent the conservative grassroots into a tailspin, unleashing a flood of angry calls from constituents into the offices of the five public nos—the truest sign yet that the tables were turning.

Former Representative Mark Meadows even called Fox News' Sean Hannity and begged him to remain neutral in the fight. Hannity refused and told Meadows that he was backing Kevin—a sea change from 2015 when Hannity's interview with Kevin spelled the beginning of the end for our first bid.

To add insult to injury, Meadows's former boss, Donald Trump, endorsed Kevin shortly thereafter in his own interview with Breitbart.

"I think it's a very dangerous game that's being played. It's a very dangerous game. Some bad things could happen," Trump stated, picking up on the doomsday narrative that we had helped sow.

"Kevin has worked very hard," Trump concluded, "I think he deserves the shot."

* * *

On December 7, Tim Reitz, executive director of the Freedom Caucus, texted me.

"Hey would it be possible to arrange a meeting with [Scott] Perry and a small number of other HFC members tomorrow late morning or early afternoon?" he asked. "Think it would be healthy to discuss where we're at right now before we leave."

Sensing a possible breakthrough, we happily agreed to schedule the meeting, hopeful that this new request by the Freedom Caucus to empower a smaller subset of members would prove more fruitful to negotiations. Kevin asked that we include Jim Jordan, as well, to help balance out Scott Perry, the gruff Freedom Caucus chair who seemed unwilling or unable to close a deal on the final points of contention.

A retired US Army brigadier general, Perry was a neat encapsulation of the anger embodied by the Freedom Caucus. That extended to his physical appearance, as well, with Perry sporting a high-and-tight buzz cut during his early years in Congress until Kevin encouraged him to grow out his hair after a closer-than-expected general election in his Harrisburg area district.

"It will help you not look so angry," Kevin explained.

Perry obliged, and his margins of victory managed to grow—along with his graying locks.

Though he and Kevin had known each other since their days as Young Republicans, the two could not have been more dissimilar when it came to temperament. In my decade plus of working for Kevin, I can count on one hand the number of times he truly lost his patience with someone—even though many certainly deserved it. But Scott Perry possessed an uncanny ability to trigger a reaction from him, which made any meeting between the two a powder keg.

"You know, this really isn't that fun for me!" Scott had yelled at the end of one particularly tense exchange in Kevin's office just a few weeks prior.

"Me neither," Kevin shot back. "So let's get it over with."

* * *

At that point, the last true sticking point in our eyes was the Motion to Vacate. As you will recall, this was the procedural mechanism by which any member of the House could trigger a vote to remove the Speaker, the modern-day equivalent of the sword of Damocles that could spell instant doom for any Speaker attempting to lead the House.

The motion seemingly came up in every one of our conversations with the holdouts—not a coincidence given who many of them were looking to for guidance: Mark Meadows, the original bomb thrower himself.

Shortly after the midterms, Meadows's Conservative Policy Institute (CPI) hosted its own new-member orientation for members of the Freedom Caucus. This was the first such session of its kind, giving Meadows and CPI a platform to indoctrinate the incoming HFC freshmen on a variety of topics, from campaigning and procedural tactics to legislative and oversight goals.

But Meadows's baby—his calling card—was the Motion to Vacate, the same one he weaponized against Speaker Boehner. And he made sure that all of his new foot soldiers were well aware of its importance.

It didn't help that Meadows and Kevin had their own tortured past, tracing back to Kevin's 2015 bid that was partially sunk by the North Carolinian.

While Kevin's much-discussed elevation of Jim Jordan to lead the Oversight Committee served to briefly thaw relations between leadership and the Freedom Caucus, what is less well known is that this move was done at the expense of Meadows, who was originally seeking the position of ranking member at that time. Instead, Meadows was denied the promotion he craved before he could even give his presentation to the Steering Committee.

Later, Kevin tried unsuccessfully to block Meadows from another promotion, that of White House chief of staff to President Trump. When Meadows was eventually brought over to serve as Trump's fourth chief, his and Kevin's rivalry simply ratcheted up even further, with the two bumping heads on a daily and weekly basis as they sought to steer the president on policy and political matters.

In that context, 2022 was just the latest in a long string of tit-for-tats between the two politicians.

* * *

We repeatedly asked for a list of members the Freedom Caucus would be sending to the meeting, only to receive back crickets. The reason why quickly became clear when Scott Perry strode into our office flanked by Florida Representative Matt Gaetz.

Though not technically a member of the Freedom Caucus, Gaetz dominated the conversation for their group from the jump and continued to bring the discussion back to the Motion to Vacate.

"We cannot begin to negotiate unless the one-person Jeffersonian Motion to Vacate is restored," he insisted, misattributing the motion to the original author of the House Rules, Thomas Jefferson. "That is the starting point, not the ending point."

As previously discussed, the Motion to Vacate was not mentioned in the House Rules until 1910, when then-Speaker Joseph Cannon created the process as a means of daring certain rebellious members inside his own party who had been agitating to strip away his vast powers. Ultimately, Speaker Cannon called their bluff and prevailed in the vote—leaving the arcane motion to sit largely dormant for over a century until it found its lively second act with Meadows and Speaker Boehner.

As I researched and learned more about this history, it made me feel slightly better to know that such intraparty squabbles have been occurring since the dawn of the republic. Even so, I would put our class of crazy up against that of any prior eras, with Gaetz being a no-brainer first overall pick.

Nevertheless, Gaetz was not stupid. He could sense that we were holding back on making any compromise on the Motion to Vacate until the very end so that it could be preserved as leverage to close a final deal. And in much the same way that we remained skeptical of Perry's ability to close a deal, Gaetz's presence also signaled to us that he harbored his own doubts in Perry's negotiation skills, which explained why he felt the need to ambush the meeting.

As Gaetz continued his diatribe, he turned to the newest recruit into his Never Kevin camp, South Carolina Representative Ralph Norman.

"Ralph, would you say restoring the Motion to Vacate is *necessary but not sufficient* for your support for Speaker?"

"*Necessary but not sufficient*" was one of Gaetz's favorite phrases—a faux lawyerly construction that he thought made him sound smart and probably went right over Norman's head, but it did not prevent Norman from nodding along "yes."

"Matt, people will never go for that," Kevin replied.

"Are you saying you'll never go for a one-person Motion to Vacate?" Gaetz pressed.

"I'm saying there's enough people in our conference who won't vote for the rules if that is included," Kevin replied. "I think we could get them down to a lower number than half the conference, but not one."

"I believe it needs to be a number that fits on one hand," Gaetz rebutted. "Or else there's enough votes on this side to deny you from being Speaker."

"It's never been used before. It would be so unprecedented," Jim Jordan tried to interject. "None of us here ever want to use something like this."

Several in the room nodded in agreement, including Chip Roy.

"Matt, do you feel the same?" Kevin asked Gaetz.

"I would only ever use the Motion to Vacate if I felt that something was done that betrayed the trust of my constituents," a loophole so subjective you could drive a Mack truck through it.

"Well, I've told you where I am and where I think the conference is," Kevin concluded. "So if that's your position, I don't think we're going to get anywhere."

* * *

"I think they just want to fight," Kevin observed to a few of our key staffers after the meeting had cleared. "I don't think they're ever going to get there."

"At least Ralph left the door open," I said, trying to keep the attitude among the team positive. "I think there's room here."

"Yeah, but you saw how depressed Jim was," Kevin said. "Even he doesn't know how to get through to them."

Inevitably, our conversation also circled back to the Motion to Vacate, which Kevin was loath to accept having seen firsthand the torment that it inflicted upon Speakers Boehner and Ryan. Yet giving on this ask also seemed to be the only surefire way to break the current Freedom Caucus logjam—leaving us between a true rock and a hard place.

That day, Kevin was particularly piqued by a comment made during one of the organizing meetings by Kentucky Representative Thomas Massie, who helped author the Motion to Vacate that Mark Meadows introduced against John Boehner.

"Guys, there are other ways to depose a Speaker besides the Motion to Vacate," Massie told the conference.

"What was Massie saying with that?" Kevin asked.

"Any Speaker without 218 isn't really a Speaker," I explained.

Simply put, the House is a majoritarian institution, through and through. Everything we do—from approving committee assignments and upholding rulings made by the Speaker to setting the annual calendar and even adjourning the House—only works if the majority party can enforce its will with the votes of 218 members.

But if the majority party ever lost its ability to corral 218 votes, all bets would be off. That extended to the question of removing a Speaker, which could effectively be achieved through other means—such as using 218 members to sign a discharge petition or overturn the ruling of the chair on the question of whether a Motion to Vacate was in order.

"That's what Massie meant," I said. "It sucks, but your job is at risk every day—Motion to Vacate or not."

* * *

Later that evening, we received a new letter signed by seven members of the Freedom Caucus, including Scott Perry, Chip Roy, Dan Bishop of North Carolina, Andrew Clyde of Georgia, Paul Gosar and Eli Crane of Arizona, and Andy Ogles of Tennessee. Chip called me right as one of our press staffers texted me a link to the letter.

"As we form the 118th Congress, any GOP Speaker candidate must make clear he or she will advance rules, policies, and an organizational structure that will result in the values listed below," the letter began.

It then went on to detail eight categories of requests—starting with, you guessed it, the Motion to Vacate.

We had been insisting for weeks that the Freedom Caucus move beyond their vague calls for "transformational change" and actually specify their demands. In that regard, this letter finally gave us something to chew on and work with.

Besides the Motion to Vacate, the list itself was not horrible. Some of the items were ones we had already planned to institute, like a firm rule providing seventy-two hours of advance notice for members to read any bills that were to be voted on.

Others were less well defined, but also in line with Kevin's stated goals—such as including broader representation on committees and uniting the conference around shared priorities that we would insist upon in negotiations with the Senate and White House, like reducing spending and securing the border.

There was also a call to stand up a new select Church Committee to investigate perceived instances of a weaponized government, modeled on the 1975 select committee led by Idaho Senator Frank Church that uncovered abuses by the CIA, FBI, NSA, and IRS. This was not an entirely novel or difficult request as even Nancy Pelosi was forced to establish a few select committees of her own in 2018 to win over detractors, including one on climate change and another on economic inequality.

"I want you to understand that this letter was written very purposefully," Chip tried to assure me. "In particular, I would draw your attention to the last sentence and how it is worded."

That last sentence read: "We believe these [requests] should form the basis of any conversation about our leadership and without regard to any one request, the totality of the requests must be addressed if we are to truly unite as a Conference."

"Explain what you mean by that," I asked.

"Everyone is focused on the Motion to Vacate. I think that's important—but it's not the whole game," Chip said. "We need all of these concerns addressed. And the greater degree to which they are addressed, the higher the threshold I think we could live with on the Motion to Vacate."

Conversely, Chip continued, the less we negotiated with them on the aforementioned areas of interest, the more fervently they would hold to the standard that any single member could trigger a Motion to Vacate.

"Understood—thanks, Chip. I appreciate the heads-up. Talk soon."

As soon as we hung up, I called Kevin to give him a readout on the conversation.

"This is a good thing," I said. "These could be their terms of surrender."

I relayed the same sentiment to our senior staff text chain.

"This letter is helpful in one key way: They've set the parameters for final negotiations," I said. "They will need to decide what's most important—changing how we do business or going after [Kevin]. But I sense they're looking for an off-ramp and need to take it when Given. Otherwise they lose all credibility."

CHAPTER 12

"JUST WIN, BABY"

"You guys will get there," one of my counterparts in Pelosi's office remarked that December. "It's just a matter of what do they ask for and can you live with it?"

"And how many ballots it takes," I added, seeking to elicit a response.

"Oh no, it's got to be on the first," he said. "If you don't win on the first, it's over."

My colleague was right to be skeptical. To that point, a Speaker's election had not gone to multiple ballots in over one hundred years—the last occurrence being in 1923 when Republican Frederick H. Gillett of Massachusetts needed nine ballots to win an outright majority. Needless to say, we were not keen on being the ones to break the streak.

To head off such a multi-ballot scenario, we looked far and wide for inspiration, even drawing some strategy advice from a sixth-century Chinese general.

"Never directly attack an opponent whose advantage is derived from their position," Wang Jingze wrote. "Instead, lure them away from their position to separate them from their source of strength."

For the Freedom Caucus, the House floor was their position of strength. Despite all that was written in the press at that time about them "not having a plan," I only felt that was partially true. In fact, at least as far as Matt Gaetz was concerned, their plan was remarkably straightforward: Go to the floor, have five people say any name other than "McCarthy" every single time, and wait for the rest of the conference to lose patience and give up.

That is why we did our best to "lure the tiger down the mountain," as the saying went. Our odds of success were much greater if we could get the holdouts in a room before January and reach an agreement behind closed doors as opposed to walking into a chaotic, unprecedented floor fight where anything could happen.

Loyal as many of our allies might have been, Congress abhorred a vacuum, and we predicted that a restless conference would only tolerate a stalemate for so long before looking elsewhere.

* * *

We continued to trade notes with the Freedom Caucus throughout the Christmas recess and hosted a conference call with members of the Five Families on December 30 to provide a status update on the House Rules package. Here, Kevin extended his biggest olive branch to date: floating a compromise of lowering the threshold for triggering a Motion to Vacate vote to any five Republican members.

News of the call quickly leaked to the press, and the response was immediate from some of the Never Kevins.

"No, less than 5!!" Ralph Norman said in a text message to CNN on the new proposed Motion to Vacate threshold. "2 or less (my opinion)."

"He's gotta get down to one," Matt Gaetz added.

Our allies responded with their own counterpressure, including a letter signed by the Republican Main Street Caucus led by Dusty Johnson of South Dakota and Stephanie Bice of Oklahoma that vowed to only agree to lowering the threshold for deposing a Speaker if doing so resulted in the holdouts voting for Kevin on the floor.

Ditto for a group of fifteen GOP members from centrist battleground districts who said they would be voting for McCarthy "regardless of how many votes it takes" and not supporting any "consensus candidate"—a letter that elicited a particularly strong response from Chip Roy, who texted me to say that it "was not helpful in tone or substance."

By now, this had become a familiar pattern to us: The Freedom Caucus could sling arrows and issue ultimatums, but the second a different corner of the conference did so, they cried foul and claimed that it threatened to erode all of our progress. In my view, this was yet another example of why you would be better off having a psychology degree to work in Congress than any education in political science or public policy.

Just before midnight, Kevin forwarded our group chain a text he received from Freedom Caucus Chair Scott Perry.

"Mr. Leader, I've attempted to contact everyone with my notes from the call today and gotten some but not others," he began. "However, the consensus from the members of the group I was able to speak with is that you should outline what you are 'giving' regarding the letter we sent to you earlier. We are being held to the content of the letter and members feel it would be a good faith effort in return if you would do the same."

Dan Meyer, Natalie Joyce, and I met with Kevin in the Capitol the next day to type out a formal response for the Freedom Caucus. We titled the document "Restoring the People's House and Ending Business as Usual" and sent it back to Perry around 3:00 p.m. on the last calendar day of 2022.

"Thank you for your letters and discussions over the recent weeks and months," it began. "I believe we share the same goals for our conference, our Congress, and our country—and I am committed to delivering on the following transformational and bold changes that have been raised."

Our response then went on to spell out nearly forty different commitments, rules changes, and other proposed reforms that we had endorsed to help unite and govern our majority. The items were categorized under three subheadings: (1) Improving the Legislative Process and Empowering Members to Represent Their Constituents; (2) Strengthening Our Republican Conference and Achieving Conservative Wins; and (3) Breaking Washington's Addiction to Spending and Holding D.C. Accountable.

For good measure, Kevin called Perry to describe the contents of the letter, and I tried to connect with Tim Reitz, only to discover that he was out of the country proposing to his girlfriend in Saint Lucia. Talk about timing, Tim!

* * *

While we were still together in the office, Kevin got a call from friend and longtime American sportscaster Jim Gray.

"Jim, I've got you on speakerphone with my staff. Tell them what you've been telling me," Kevin said.

"Just win, baby!" Gray began. "Do whatever it takes."

From there, he proceeded to uncork an invigorating pep talk, exactly what the doctor ordered at that time for our band of ragged and weary foot soldiers.

"Do you remember the scores of Tom Brady's Super Bowls? Do you remember if they went into overtime?" Gray asked, "No. You remember he won six Super Bowls—that's it."

The line brought to mind Kevin's oft-repeated mantra on his many member calls in the immediate aftermath of the disappointing midterm elections: "Do you know what they call someone who wins the Super Bowl in overtime? Super Bowl champion," Kevin told them.

"A man is not finished when he's defeated. He is finished when he quits. Do not ring the bell, do not quit," Gray said, paraphrasing former President Richard Nixon.

"We won't give up," Kevin said, as we all nodded in agreement.

"Circumstances change. Things change. What feels like it matters today might not matter tomorrow. Do what you need to do—but get in there and then make it happen," Gray concluded.

That last line, in particular, is the one that stuck with me the most. While we knew we were putting ourselves out on a limb by giving in to some of the Freedom Caucus' demands, we were not fearful of what was to come. Instead, we trusted that Kevin and our team had the skills and instincts necessary to prove the doubters wrong and excel in the job.

If that was not good enough, so be it. But unlike 2015, we were not going to shy away and live the rest of our lives with the four most dreadful words in the English language: "What could have been."

* * *

The next day, January 1, 2023, we emailed all of our members the House rules package, along with a letter from Kevin that turned the term-sheet we prepared for the Freedom Caucus into prose.

> Dear Republican Colleague,
> On Tuesday, the 118th Congress of the United States will gavel into session and Republicans will reclaim a majority in the House of Representatives after four years of Democrat rule. As our conference's nominee for Speaker of the House, the question I am asked most is: "How will you be different from past Speakers?"

The letter then detailed Kevin's governing philosophy, which included providing members with more opportunities to influence the legislative process and using his appointments on key panels to ensure committees more closely reflected the ideological makeup of our conference.

> When it comes to leading the Republican conference, I will strive to rebuild the trust that has become frayed by broken promises and unmet expectations in past majorities. . . . In short, I will work with everyone in our party to build conservative consensus and translate that consensus into action.

And, of course, it addressed the elephant in the room that was the Motion to Vacate.

> Finally, just as the Speaker is elected by the whole body, we will restore the ability for any 5 members of the majority party to initiate a vote to remove the Speaker if so warranted. This procedure was first created in 1910 during a period when Members of the House were equally frustrated by a bottled-up, top-down process controlled by then-Speaker Joseph Cannon. Cannon prevailed in that vote, but agreed to implement a series of reforms that reduced the Speaker's power in exchange.
>
> In like manner, it's time for our new Republican majority to embrace these bold reforms and move forward as one. I truly believe these transformative changes we are making will restore the People's House and end business as usual in Washington. That's why on January 3—and every day thereafter—I stand ready to be judged not by my words, but by my actions as Speaker.

Like many other kids around the country, my first visit to our nation's capital was on the eighth grade field trip—pictured here with my mother, who served as a class chaperone. Even then, I felt a certain reverence and awe for both the history of DC and the people who made our government run on a daily basis. When I began to contemplate where to move after college graduation, it was an easy choice to return to the city that I first fell in love with all those years ago. *Author photograph.*

I can still remember riding up the Capitol South metro escalator in April 2012, wearing my least ill-fitting suit, and grasping a slip of paper with the name of a California congressman I had never met: "Rep. Kevin McCarthy." Little did I know, that ten-week internship in the Majority Whip's office would lead to a ten-plus year career on Capitol Hill—with more twists and turns than I could have ever predicted. *Author photograph.*

In the wake of the 2008 elections, Republicans needed a rebrand to signal a clean break from the past. Enter the "Young Guns," a nickname coined by Fred Barnes of *The Weekly Standard* in his profile of three rising conservative lawmakers: Eric Cantor, the leader (*left*); Paul Ryan, the thinker (*right*); and Kevin McCarthy, the strategist. *Getty Images.*

Less than a year after I began working in Washington, I experienced my first political earthquake: the defeat of Majority Leader Eric Cantor. The powerful Virginia lawmaker was not only one of Kevin's closest friends but was widely presumed to be the next Speaker of the House. Cantor's unexpected loss created a vacancy in the number-two slot, which Kevin ran for and won handily—putting us on a collision course with the "Curse of the Majority Leader." *Getty Images.*

The day after Pope Francis's visit to the Capitol in 2015, Speaker John Boehner announced his resignation—leading to Kevin's first bid for the post that was ultimately abandoned. Years later, the Pope told Kevin that he and his staff watched all fifteen ballots of 2023 from his personal offices in the Vatican. *Getty Images.*

It was not a long conversation when Kevin pulled me into his office to offer me the position of floor director—the job I had most aspired to since first interning on Capitol Hill. The promotion made me the youngest floor director in House history at age twenty-five and elevated me into his innermost circle of trusted senior staff. *Caleb Smith.*

Only two years later, Republicans lost the House and found ourselves in the minority—easily my least favorite pit stop in Washington. The minority did create some interesting new dynamics, however, with formerly bitter enemies in the party now suddenly unified in fighting against the Democratic majority. *Caleb Smith.*

In 2016, I met a young clerk for the Energy and Commerce Committee named Giulia Giannangeli at Speaker Paul Ryan's Christmas party. We hit it off immediately and gradually fell in love—a classic Hill romance. I proposed to her on the eastern shore of Saint Michaels, Maryland, in October 2020, and we were married a year later at St. Joseph's Catholic Church on Capitol Hill. *Stacey Moua Photography*.

When I entered the War Room on election night 2022, it was immediately clear to me that all was not well. As you can tell by the look on my face, even if we managed to take back the House, I knew that our incredibly slim margins meant that we were all in for a long slog until January. *Keenan Hochschild.*

One of my roles in the office was to prepare suggested talking points and slides for Kevin to use ahead of critical party meetings. While he was a little unsure when we showed him the quote from Don Corleone in *The Godfather*, it thankfully had the intended effect in the meeting—breaking the ice and leading to the creation of a new subset of members known as "The Five Families." *Caleb Smith.*

There were certain mornings working on the Hill when you did not need an alarm clock to wake up. As soon as your brain registered even an ounce of consciousness, your eyes sprang open and your body clicked into "go mode." That is where I found myself on the morning of January 3, hours before the first official party meeting of the 118th Congress and the first day of floor balloting for Speaker. *Caleb Smith.*

A Speaker's election had not gone to multiple ballots in over a century, forcing us to think creatively about how to keep our block of 200 supporters intact while breaking the twenty holdouts. In the end, it would be the longest contest for the position the House had seen since the Civil War. *U.S. House Office of Photography.*

Throughout the week, we relied on key allies and surrogates to advocate on our behalf and keep the broader membership apprised of where things stood. While countless members aided in this endeavor, few were as impactful or tenacious as North Carolina Representative Patrick McHenry (*top left*) and Louisiana Representative Garret Graves (*bottom right*). Later, Kevin tapped both McHenry and Graves to serve as his lead negotiators with the Biden White House as we worked to raise the debt ceiling. The resulting legislation, the Fiscal Responsibility Act, represented the largest deficit reduction bill enacted in a generation. *U.S. House Office of Photography.*

Although Texas Representative Chip Roy was not the elected chair of the House Freedom Caucus, it seemed clear to me that he was the true center of gravity of the group. I believed that if we could get Chip to commit to Kevin, the other Maybe Kevins would fall in line too—and I made it my personal mission to deliver his vote. *U.S. House Office of Photography.*

One member who had no interest in being helpful was Florida Representative Matt Gaetz—leader of the Never Kevin cohort. We agreed that keeping him away was our best shot to whittle down the opposition—a "cancer that needs to be extracted." Though Gaetz has denied the allegations, the House Ethics Committee later found substantial evidence that the disgraced former congressman paid thousands of dollars to women for sex, including a 17-year-old. *U.S. House Office of Photography.*

That Friday, I could not find the tie I wanted to wear so I reached for my next best option: a bright orange tie that I would typically don on the rare Mondays that followed a Chicago Bears victory. *We're not gonna win today anyways,* I told myself as I looped the admittedly loud-colored tie around my neck—one that would eventually turn me into a meme known as "Orange Tie Guy." *U.S. House Office of Photography.*

Although I wanted to punch Matt Gaetz in the face for reneging on his deal and trying to twist my words, I was not about to let him use me as an excuse to cause even more of a scene. Instead, I said my piece and then backed away to allow the members to try to sort it out among themselves. That was right about when a few other members decided they wanted a word with Gaetz, too, causing quite the commotion. *Getty Images*.

As soon as I heard the last holdouts relay that they were finally ready to vote present, my attention immediately turned to defeating the motion to adjourn. "Vote no! Vote no!" I screamed, running up the aisle and pointing my thumb downwards. *Keenan Hochschild.*

Fortunately, our members did not need much urging, and a stampede of Republicans flooded the well to grab red voting cards, signaling their change of vote and giving us a dramatic new lease on life. *U.S. House Office of Photography.*

Throughout the week, Kevin and I would emotionally seesaw off one another. Anytime I would start to get down, he would buck me up and vice versa. After we won and the mob of members wishing congratulations had died down, I was finally able to utter the two words I had been waiting to say for over a decade: "Mr. Speaker." It was a moment I will never forget. *Top: U.S. House Office of Photography. Bottom: Keenan Hochschild.*

With the winning votes secured, I finally had a chance to roam the floor, where members offered their congratulations to our team, along with hugs left and right. The most meaningful embraces, though, were with my wife, Giulia, and the members of our floor team and senior staff—particularly Natalie Joyce (*left*) and Matt Sparks (*center*). The three of us had been on this ride together for over a decade and made it out on the other side alive. *Caleb Smith.*

The day Mike Johnson was elected Speaker was a date that I had circled on my personal calendar for months. After my brother was ordained a priest, Kevin's gift to him was an invitation to give the opening prayer for the House on October 25, 2023. Kevin formally introduced Father Jeremy Leganski at noon, the last time he would ever be atop the Speaker's rostrum. Meanwhile, I bowed my head and wept as my brother led the House in prayer, with my dad and in-laws watching from the gallery and Giulia draping her arm around me for support. That, too, would be the last day I would ever walk the House floor. *Keenan Hochschild*.

* * *

That evening, after I said my prayers at the 6:30 p.m. mass at St. Vincent de Paul in Navy Yard, my friend AJ Sugarman invited Giulia and me to dinner with his parents and my old roommates at an upscale Indian restaurant in downtown DC. His parents—legendary Hollywood producer Burt Sugarman and renowned former host of *Entertainment Tonight* Mary Hart—were big Republican boosters and had flown into town to witness the Speaker vote as longtime friends of Kevin.

On our way over, Kevin texted that he had a good call with Matt Gaetz.

"From [Gaetz]. My suggestion, FWIW—invite Gaetz, Good, Rosendale, and Norman to all see you together tomorrow afternoon. Make your last offer—which isn't what we discussed on the call because it doesn't have the [one-person Motion to Vacate]."

That seemed like a good sign. As mentioned, allowing any one individual to call for the Motion to Vacate was something we assumed we would have to give on all along. The key was holding it until the last possible moment to close the deal so that the Freedom Caucus would not have time to ask for more. Perhaps we could secure 218 votes before going to the floor after all?

Chip Roy also called me during dinner to check in.

"What are we doing with Vacate?" he asked.

"I am just speaking for myself here, but I feel pretty confident that Kevin will go down to one if that seals the deal," I relayed.

"Okay, so Motion to Vacate is at five right now but can be one. And what about the Rules Committee?" he asked.

This was a late-breaking ask from the Freedom Caucus. The House Rules Committee was a small yet influential panel charged with determining what amendments would be made in order and how much debate would be allotted to bills coming to the floor. All nine of the majority party's selections were hand-picked by the Speaker, while the four minority slots were chosen by the House minority leader.

"We need two or three seats on Rules," Chip said.

While putting Freedom Caucus members on the committee was not without risk, we also felt that it could provide a useful mechanism for sniffing out issues before they spiraled out of control. After all, if the Freedom Caucus was not happy with a particular rule, any five members could just vote it down on the floor. From that standpoint, it was better for us to learn about potential objections up front at the committee level as opposed to being surprised later on and wasting precious floor time in the process.

"I think two slots is doable. I am not sure about three," I told him. "But let's talk with Kevin."

I tried to push Chip to consider where he best fit into the emerging arrangement, thinking that perhaps dangling a higher-profile role would further encourage him to play ball.

"For what it's worth, I think you would be someone excellent for Rules," I said.

"That's kind of you to say. I think there's a variety of ways I can serve," Chip replied, not showing his hand one way or another.

To his credit, Chip never explicitly asked for anything for himself. Even so, I knew that he would be a vocal and pivotal player in whatever we would venture to accomplish over the course of the Congress. And as we had learned, it was usually better to have folks inside the tent pissing out than outside pissing in.

"Fair enough. Let's get this done and then we can figure out what makes sense," I said, encouraging him to touch base with Kevin, as well.

For the first time in weeks, I actually felt like our plan was going to come to fruition. At the last minute, we would strike a deal, land the plane, and finally put an end to the drama—just as we drew it up.

I returned to the restaurant to pick at my half-eaten plate of cold tandoori.

"How did it go, Johnny?" AJ's mother asked, using my college moniker.

"We're going to get it done," I told the table. "Stay for the vote."

PART III

FIVE DAYS IN JANUARY

———

CHAPTER 13

A MODEST PROPOSAL

Despite my growing confidence, our whip count was still well short of 218 just a day before the pivotal floor vote. And since no living person was present the last time Congress experienced a multi-ballot vote for Speaker, we had to think outside the box in case an agreement was not reached with the Freedom Caucus and a Plan B was necessary to fight it out on the floor.

Our chief of staff, Dan Meyer, reasoned that the most analogous situation to ours was not that of whipping a bill, but rather that of a political nominating convention. Though brokered conventions at the presidential level have all but disappeared over the past forty years, they were still a regular occurrence at the state level, including in Dan's home state of Minnesota, where candidates for office would often need to advance through multiple ballots in order to receive the state party's endorsement.

With that concept in mind, Dan arranged a phone call with an old boss of his—former Republican Congressman Vin Weber of Minnesota—who had run several such delegate-counting operations over the years. Pound for pound, it was probably the single most important call in terms of strategy we would have in the lead-up to January.

In particular, Weber offered three key pieces of advice.

For starters, there was the question of where Kevin ought to sit. Traditionally, candidates for Speaker would stay away from the floor during the votes, even abstaining from the vote entirely when it was clear that they already had enough votes to win.

While we obviously would not have that luxury this time around, we initially thought it would make sense to keep Kevin physically situated in the Republican cloakroom or somewhere else off the floor so we could bring back any recalcitrant members to talk with him in private. Weber quickly talked us out of that plan.

"Always have the candidate be visible and seen," he explained. "It's much harder to screw someone over when they're sitting twenty feet away from you."

Second, Weber implored us to "be more organized than the opposition." This could take a variety of forms, like enlisting allies to serve as babysitters to keep track of any wavering members. Better yet, spread these spotters around the floor to sniff out and tamp down any pockets of dissent. Weber even suggested we go so far as to have our allies accompany the detractors on their walk over from their office to the floor.

"Make sure the last voice in their head before the vote is a positive one," he instructed.

The third and final piece of advice was the most important: "Never let an alternate candidate pick up steam."

"If that happens," Weber warned, "you have real problems."

* * *

To date, we had done fairly well in our effort to deny oxygen to any would-be challengers.

As discussed, the most frequent alternative mentioned to Kevin was his second-in-command, Majority Leader Steve Scalise. The Louisianan's shadow candidacy was detailed in a late December *Politico* Playbook column titled "Speaker Scalise?" and further stoked by a series of anonymous quotes that pegged him as the next man up.

"If at some point, if Kevin did take his name out, then you would have good people [running]," one unnamed GOP lawmaker told CNN that December. "Scalise would probably be the guy."

Another Republican source added, "If Kevin doesn't get it, Scalise gets it easily."

The other member who seemed viable on paper—and who I actually thought stood a better chance were Kevin to falter—was our foe turned friend Jim Jordan of Ohio. Still beloved by the grassroots, Jim could easily count on the votes of the Freedom Caucus while remaining palatable to the center of our conference following his successful stints atop the Oversight and Judiciary Committees.

To Jim's credit, he was unwavering in his public backing of Kevin, flatly telling CNN "no" when asked if he would run for Speaker if Kevin could not get the votes.

"I want to chair the Judiciary Committee," Jim said repeatedly.

To be safe, we continued to take pains to keep both men close. For instance, while custom dictated that Conference Chair Elise Stefanik of New York would give the first speech to enter Kevin's name into nomination on the floor, we determined then and there on the phone with Weber that we would ask Jordan to give the second nominating speech should one be necessary, followed by Scalise, so as to further drive home the point that no daylight existed among the three.

Along the same lines, we probed Weber on what he thought of our idea of naming Jordan as "Assistant Speaker" as an olive branch to the right. He thought it was a good idea and a sound strategy to ensure all roads ran through Kevin and Kevin alone.

At the end of the call, I finally mustered the courage to ask the question that was really on my mind: "What are our odds?"

"I'd say 60/40," Weber answered.

Shit, that is not what I was hoping to hear, I thought to myself.

"You're closer to the situation than I am, and maybe the odds are slightly better," he said. "But that's about what I'd put it at."

I was hoping he would have said 70/30 or even 80/20. But taking a step back, it was hard to argue with Weber's conclusion. While Kevin was the clear front-runner and had performed a Herculean task just to stay afloat these last two months, we were still staring at a sheet of paper that had twenty members in the no or undecided column just one day before the floor vote, far more than the five defections that had been publicly reported.

Kevin was equally realistic about the situation when I spoke with him later that day.

"I think they want to fight," Kevin texted in response to a particularly inflammatory tweet from Freedom Caucus Chair Scott Perry.

"Maybe. I sort of feel like they're not gonna close until the very last minute," I replied. "And any minute we close sooner is just more time they can ask for shit."

"This makes it harder for them to close," he responded, again referencing the tweet.

"Yes," I said. "We'll be prepared regardless."

* * *

Attempting to heed Weber's advice to be more organized than the opposition, we arranged an in-person meeting with the members of Kevin's whip team on the afternoon of January 2.

By that point, we had moved into the Speaker's official suite of offices, a series of ornately painted rooms just steps away from the grand rotunda that date back to the earliest days of the Capitol—including the famous "Speaker's Balcony" that boasted arguably the best views of the entire city of Washington, DC.

On second thought, "moved in" might have been a generous description given that we barely had more than our individual desks and phones set up. In fact, I never fully unpacked my things, partly out of superstition and partly out of practicality.

While I certainly did not want to jinx us, I also wanted to avoid repacking everything if the vote did not work out in our favor. Instead, the only personal item I pulled out was a medium-size whiteboard that listed the breakdown of the House majority and a single word written in red Magic Marker: "BELIEVE."

Kevin only brought out a few items, as well, but he made sure to hang three large canvas portraits painted by artist Steve Penley that had accompanied him in each of his leadership offices: a monochrome portrait of Abraham Lincoln, a brightly colored portrait of a smiling Ronald Reagan, and a massive contemporary rendition of Washington Crossing the Delaware that took up an entire wall in the main conference room and overlooked the assembled group that day.

We squeezed over thirty members into every nook and cranny of the room, each more supportive and fired up than the last, including Carlos Gimenez of

Florida, Mike Lawler of New York, and Jason Smith of Missouri, to name a few. Everyone told Kevin that they were in it for the long haul and that they would never be voting for anyone else.

"I don't care what happens; I am never going anywhere," Kevin began, prompting a vigorous round of applause around the table.

We walked the group through a minute-by-minute timeline of the following day when the first floor ballots would occur before pulling up a diagram of the House floor that we had divided into several numbered sections. Each member was assigned either a designated zone to sit in or a specific member to keep track of, ensuring we had full coverage across the floor. Everyone was also added to a text platform that we would use for communicating updates throughout the balloting.

Just as the meeting with our allies was wrapping, Matt Gaetz, Scott Perry, and Lauren Boebert of Colorado arrived for a meeting with Kevin. Based on our communications with Chip and Gaetz the day prior, it was fair to assume this could be the meeting to finally seal a deal, with Gaetz remarking to the press on his way into the office that we might have been "on the verge of a New Year's miracle."

Unfortunately, the ball drop would need to wait a little bit longer.

* * *

Gaetz led off the meeting for the holdouts.

"Mr. Leader, we have been working very hard all day to put this together," he began. "I believe what we have here is a proposal that can get you 218 or maybe even 219 votes."

Kevin and our team listened intently, waiting for the inevitable *"but . . ."*.

"Now, I know you are going to say that we are moving the goalposts," Gaetz continued. "But if you recall, I said that reducing the Motion to Vacate to one member was a precondition for beginning negotiations, not ending them. And so we have only been able to put this together after you indicated yesterday that the one-person Motion to Vacate would be acceptable."

There's the but, I thought.

"I cannot give you this as it is our only copy, but I will read it for you now," Gaetz said, nervously riffling to the first in a stack of what looked like at least five or six pages.

The list began innocuously enough, restating many of the same rules changes that we had already publicly committed to in the House Rules package, as well as a handful of bills that they wanted to see move. But by page three or four, I think I literally blacked out in anger and understood what it meant when you said something made your "blood boil."

Incredibly, Gaetz began to list off dozens of premier committee assignments for specific members of the Freedom Caucus and demanded that each of these assignments be approved by the Steering Committee before going to the floor to vote for Speaker. As if that were not egregious enough, they also demanded that Freedom Caucus members be named the chairs of various subcommittees and full committees—starting, of course, with the three members in the room.

"Matt Gaetz will be the chair of the Armed Services subcommittee on Military Personnel. Lauren Boebert will be chair of the Natural Resources subcommittee on Energy and Mineral Resources. Scott Perry will be the chairman of the Church Committee on the Weaponization of Government, which will be its own Select Committee—not a subcommittee of Judiciary—and will have a budget equal to that of the January 6th Select Committee," he continued.

The list only went downhill from there, including a demand that Freedom Caucus Members be given four seats on the Rules Committee. As mentioned, there were only nine total seats for the majority party on this panel, and we had discussed naming up to two Freedom Caucus Members a few hours before, with the possibility for a third Freedom Caucus–adjacent member.

Gaetz also gave himself another appointment, heading up a new House legal action group that would be stacked with Freedom Caucus members. In theory, its purpose would have been to file lawsuits against the administration. But underneath the surface, it seemed like he was trying to carve out a blocking and tackling mechanism to protect himself—a taxpayer-subsidized legal defense fund, if you will.

The final bullet on the document was a stipulation that "no retaliation" could be levied against any of the members who were involved in the effort to block Kevin.

"We know that you may attempt to circumvent us and move that the election be conducted based on plurality, with the threat that doing so might elect a Democrat Speaker," Gaetz concluded, alluding to a hypothetical scenario that we never seriously contemplated as doing so would have required getting Democrats to vote for a change in the rules. "If so, we are prepared to vote against you, elect Hakeem Jeffries as Speaker, and lead the opposition to him for the next two years."

When he finally finished reading, there was a tense awkward silence before Kevin chose to respond.

"It sounds like you just want to be Speaker," Kevin told him.

"But you would get the portrait," Gaetz replied.

"I have plenty of pictures of myself. I don't need a fucking portrait. Get out."

With that, the three stood up and left, and we sat there flabbergasted. It is the only meeting in Washington that I wish had been tape-recorded because it would have shown how truly unreasonable and out of touch these people were.

* * *

After the trio had departed, Kevin and a few members of our senior staff remained in his office to try to digest what just happened.

"That was not an offer meant to be taken seriously," our chief, Dan Meyer, said, noting among many flaws in their plan that we would have an actual revolt on our hands if we tried to get the conference to sign off on plum positions for the Freedom Caucus before going to the floor.

"Moving the goalposts?" I laughed. "That's moving to an entire new zip code!"

Kevin was pissed off, but more incredulous than anything.

"We're going to war now," he told us. "Fuck 'em."

On my walk home, I texted Chip.

"Are you a part of this Gaetz 'offer'? Him, Perry, and Boebert came by," I said.

He didn't respond until three hours later, first with a text and then a phone call around 11 p.m.

"Dude, where were you? Did you know that's what they were going to present?" I asked him.

He gave an excuse for why he couldn't be there and then played dumb as to the details of what Gaetz presented.

"To be honest," I told him, "I feel like this entire thing has been a giant waste of time."

"John, I understand that you feel that way and I am sorry. I promise you that everything I have done has been in good faith," he said.

"You guys just don't know how to say yes. If you can't say yes to what we're offering, I am not sure how we can expect to accomplish anything this Congress," I replied.

"What I would have said to that if I were you is: 'Okay, that is aggressive—how about we do X instead?'" Chip suggested in an attempt to reel things back in.

"Chip, I think we're past that point. Kevin says we're going to war," I said.

"Kevin texted me that, as well. I do not believe that will be productive," he replied. "But listen, there will come a time on the floor tomorrow when a break in the action occurs. I am just asking that you take a deep breath, count to ten, and try to see that cooler heads prevail. Be a voice of reason out there."

"I'll try, but it sounds like you made a blood oath with this group and were always going to be tied to them," I said. "I am asking you to be a leader and steer this group."

Afterward, I texted Kevin a readout of the conversation.

"I guess positives are that he still wants to hash something out. But cons are that none of them are willing to actually go out on a limb to make a deal," I said.

"Fuck them," Kevin replied.

"Try to get some rest," I concluded. "That's my final update for the evening."

CHAPTER 14

JANUARY 3, 2023—"WE'RE GOING TO WAR"

There were certain mornings working on the Hill when you did not need an alarm clock to wake you up. As soon as your brain registered even an ounce of consciousness, your eyes sprang open and your body clicked into "go mode." That is where I found myself at daybreak on the morning of January 3.

Members of the House Republican Conference would meet a few hours later for the first official party meeting of the 118th Congress. And for the first time in four years, the meeting would take place in HC-5, the room reserved for use by the majority party in the basement of the Capitol, near the original planned resting site of George Washington and only feet away from the hallway that the President-elect walks down before taking the oath of office on Inauguration Day on the East Front.

As mentioned, one of my jobs was to prepare suggested talking points for Kevin ahead of these party meetings. And over the course of my ten-plus years in the office, we had developed a pretty good rapport that involved the floor team and Kevin arriving to the Capitol at around 7:30 or 8 a.m. to review a first cut of the slides and talkers that we had prepared the night before.

On good days, Kevin would sign off with maybe a few minor tweaks, and we would be set. On more exciting days, he would propose an entirely different vision for what his message ought to be and have us start from scratch—only now with even less time to put it together. I think he secretly enjoyed coming up with an idea for a new graphic, chart, or video with as little time remaining before the meeting as possible, simply to see us sweat in trying to pull it off.

That morning, a single phrase rung out in my head: "The truth will set you free." In practical terms, that meant telling our members the truth and exposing the Freedom Caucus' absurd "offer" from the night before for everyone to see. I texted my deputy, Chris Bien, to get in early because we had some new slides to make.

"Everything we accepted over the past two months," I asked him. "All the conference rules changes. All the House rules changes. Our commitments on making committees and the leadership table more reflective of and responsive to the conference. Our target goals on spending and must-pass bills. Put it all on there."

Our senior staff all felt the same.

"I think that's the right venue. And a strong message," Matt Sparks responded on our group thread.

"I agree," Dan Meyer added. "I think their strategy is to surprise people with how many votes are against Kevin. So we have to prepare our people and manage expectations on that first ballot and radicalize them against these people who are now demanding personal swampy requests. Voting with them is not just voting against Kevin—it's voting for Gaetz, Boebert, and Perry's final offer being gavels for each of them."

Natalie Joyce concurred: "Agree. He should ask Perry and Gaetz to make the offer before the conference because we need buy in. No Speaker can deliver this on their own. We've negotiated for weeks to get members in [a] good spot with [their] other offer. Then if they don't, Kevin reads broadly through their demands."

We fed all that into Kevin, who in turn texted Gaetz, Perry, and Boebert.

"Thanks for the meeting last night," he said to the trio. "I couldn't implement anything you requested without the support of the conference, so I have reserved time for you to present it to the conference this morning."

"Does that mean the offer is being accepted?" Gaetz replied.

* * *

During our prep session that morning, we showed Kevin our newly made slide deck listing all the items the Freedom Caucus had requested and received over recent months with a green check mark next to each.

"Don't be angry in there," I advised. "Just walk through the items and show that you've been eminently reasonable."

To reinforce the point on tone, we jokingly showed Kevin the clip of Will Ferrell from *Old School* after he caught fire during the gymnastics event: "We can't have anyone freak out out there! We've gotta keep our composure. We've come too far. There's too much to lose," Ferrell screamed as he slammed a folding chair against a wall of lockers. "We've gotta keep our composure!"

On his way down to the meeting, Kevin bumped into Mike Rogers of Alabama, a senior member of the party and the incoming chair of the Armed Services Committee with purview over the Pentagon. I could not hear their conversation, but Rogers was clearly rip-shit angry. Kevin did not do much to calm him down, perhaps a foreshadowing of what was to come.

Admittedly, I was feeling pretty jacked up, as well, and fired off a text to Chip.

"You've overplayed your hand," I said as I walked into HC-5.

* * *

At 8:58 a.m., the room was packed to the gills, a rarity given that our party meetings rarely, if ever, started on time. We began with the customary prayer and the Pledge of Allegiance before turning to leadership reports at the top of the agenda. Majority Leader Steve Scalise presented first, followed by Majority Whip Tom Emmer, and then Kevin was recognized to close.

For the first half of his remarks, Kevin heeded our advice, calmly going item by item, smiling, and saying how we had worked in good faith to accept so many of the proposed ideas. But then, something snapped. And instead of Will Ferrell, Kevin turned into Leonardo DiCaprio from *The Wolf of Wall Street* in the "I'm not fuckin' leaving!" scene.

Unsurprisingly, Gaetz did not accept time to present his group's proposed offer to the broader membership. So Kevin chose to do it for them, outlining some of the more egregious asks they requested the night prior.

"These people came and asked for things not for the conference, but for themselves personally," Kevin boomed. "HELL NO am I taking that deal!"

The conference erupted in a standing ovation, the pent-up tension and anger in the room palpable.

"There might be ten, fifteen, even twenty people that don't want to vote for me," Kevin went on, trying to get ahead of the larger-than-anticipated number of defections we were planning for. "But I am never leaving."

"I don't care if I have to find out who my last five friends are here. I earned this job, we won this majority, and we're gonna win this vote, dammit!" he roared, triggering another boisterous standing ovation.

* * *

After leadership reports, we turned to the portion of the meeting known as "open mic," where any member could come forward and speak to the conference for one minute apiece.

Our member services director, Natalie Joyce, had worked with our allies to flood the mics, a common strategy we would use ahead of big conference meetings. But no one needed much encouragement that morning as the rush of lawmakers to the two standing microphones on each side of the room was swift and immediate.

Armed Services Chair Mike Rogers of Alabama was first to speak.

"I'm on the Steering Committee, and if these holdouts don't want to support the nominee, that's fine," Rogers shouted. "They just won't get committee assignments. That's the way it'll work!"

While Rogers's comments received applause inside the room, they sent the Freedom Caucus into a downright tizzy. Individuals we had marked down as being on the fence began to shake their heads in disgust and leave the room as member after member took to the mic to excoriate the Freedom Caucus and their tactics.

Houston, we have a problem, I thought to myself.

After about thirty minutes of taking a beating, I noticed Chip walk into the back annex of the room with a group of his fellow holdouts. I followed him to try to calm the waters.

"Chip, you know we can go to one on the Motion to Vacate," I said, referring to the still-unfinalized question of what threshold should trigger the procedural motion. "You gotta get them to say yes before noon."

"I can't," he said, sounding defeated.

"This is as good as it's going to get, man. C'mon, we can get this done," I said, putting both of my hands on his shoulders.

"John, I can't! I've tried, but they won't listen," he continued.

With that, his eyes began to well with tears.

"Look, now I'm turning into John Boehner," Chip sighed, referring to the famously teary-eyed former Speaker.

I sensed that he was truly in turmoil, having helped light the fire for this ordeal that he was now powerless to extinguish.

* * *

As this was occurring, Freedom Caucus Chair Scott Perry was gathering some of his members in the hallway behind HC-5 for an impromptu press conference to outline their continued opposition to Kevin. Having failed with Chip, I tried my luck with Perry.

"Chairman, what more do you guys want?" I said.

"Everything in the letter!" he screamed.

"Okay, let's go over the letter. Seventy-two hours, you got it. Single subject and germaneness, you got it. Church Committee, you got it. Motion to Vacate . . ." I trailed off, remembering that we had not publicly agreed to the one-person threshold quite yet.

"Yeah, where the hell is that!?" he countered.

"We will go to one. You know that," I said.

Perry struggled to hold eye contact, as well. He was as uncomfortable as Chip, wearing the same look as when he told Kevin a few weeks earlier that this was not very fun for him. Alas, he had painted himself into a corner, too, and now could not find a way out.

"It shouldn't have taken this long, John," he said before walking around the corner to begin the presser.

* * *

On the surface, the meeting was an abject disaster. We had declared war on the notoriously emotionally fragile Freedom Caucus, and they were now more pissed off and resolute in their opposition than when they first entered the room.

"He [McCarthy] just burned himself. He just solidified fifteen or twenty who were against him," Chip Roy told Fox News later that day, specifically referencing the Mike Rogers threat to boot Freedom Caucus members from their committees.

In retrospect, however, the meeting was one of the best things that could have happened to us. Returning to the mantra that McHenry and I repeated to one another—"Hold the two hundred. Break the twenty"—we had made the shirts-versus-skins fight crystal clear, always an important element in congressional politics.

While there were certainly a few members who may not have loved Kevin and sensed an opportunity to knife him, doing so at that time would have required they stick their heads up and side with Matt Gaetz, an exponentially uglier proposition after the details of his offer were shared with the entire membership.

Intentionally or not, the two hundred were now more firmly behind us than ever before, a group that we would need to hold together if we had any shot of sustaining the first multi-ballot Speaker's election in a century.

* * *

With noon quickly approaching, the question on everyone's mind in Washington was if we were actually going to go through with taking the vote to the floor.

The truth is that we really did not have much of a choice. On the first day of a new Congress, there were no set rules established, which meant we did not have the authority to declare a recess.

Instead, the House would open at noon with the prayer and Pledge of Allegiance. A quorum call would then occur where all members recorded their presence to establish a working quorum of 218 representatives. Finally, the House would turn to electing a Speaker—the highest order of business in the House as one of the few requirements spelled out in the Constitution, necessary for filling out the presidential line of succession.

Nothing else could occur until a Speaker was elected—no legislation debated, no committees assigned, no nothing.

I confirmed this unfortunate reality in several lengthy meetings with the House Parliamentarians in the lead-up to January.

Situated just steps away from the House floor, "the Parls" were a veritable fountain of knowledge to members and staff, alike. Led by House Parliamentarian Jason Smith, this small group of lawyers served as the official nonpartisan umpires of the institution, calling procedural balls and strikes and enforcing the longstanding precedents and rules of the House.

In fact, I often equated the position of House Parliamentarian to Dumbledore from Harry Potter: someone who always had the right answer, so long as you asked the right question.

Aside from voting for Speaker, the Parls relayed that only two motions were in order: adjourning the House to a date and time certain, or proposing a change to the rules or process by which the Speaker's election would proceed.

For example, they uncovered that during one particularly deadlocked contest in the 1800s, a member proposed that the House simply elect a Speaker "by lots"—as in, put names in a hat and pick one out to be Speaker. While that particular rule change never received a vote, there were several times over the course of the week where I thought that might be the only way to resolve our impasse.

As for what happened to Kevin after the first ballot, prognostications from the punditry class were grim. *Punchbowl News* reported that, "privately, some of the lawmakers closest to McCarthy continue to tell us that they don't see a path for the California Republican to win the speakership. Not on the first ballot, or the second, or any subsequent ballots."

The bulletin continued: "Some McCarthy backers—lawmakers and aides in and outside the leadership—don't believe he can or should stay on the floor for more than two rounds of votes before bowing out. One close ally of McCarthy pegged his chances of winning the speakership at 5%."

Yikes, I thought to myself reading that line. *And here I thought Vin Weber's 60/40 odds were rough.*

* * *

Much pomp and circumstance surrounded the opening day of a new Congress. The bright lights typically reserved for the president's annual State of the Union address were turned on full blast, making for sweaty brows among the members but better views for the ever-watchful TV cameras that fed into the C-SPAN broadcast.

The public gallery was packed with friends and family of the newly elected, hoping to see their loved ones take the Oath of Office and cast their first votes as elected representatives. Meanwhile, the Hill and national press corps overflowed the tiered gallery at the south end of the Chamber, typing away on their laptops directly above the Speaker's rostrum.

The day prior, our staff did a rough walk-through on the floor, assigning zones of coverage and roles for each staffer. There, it was decided that I would be the one to stay with Kevin throughout the balloting, essentially becoming a floating body guy. As such, when the clock struck noon, Kevin and I took our places in the two seats closest to the aisle before one of the long mahogany desks on the Republican right-hand side of the chamber.

As was tradition, Conference Chair Elise Stefanik of New York was recognized to give the nominating speech for Kevin. Democratic Caucus Chair Pete Aguilar of California followed, placing the name of Minority Leader Hakeem Jeffries into nomination for his party. And finally, Paul Gosar sought recognition to nominate a third candidate for speaker, his fellow Arizonan Andy Biggs, before balloting commenced.

The election of the Speaker was conducted as a "manual roll call." Unlike other votes taken in Congress that were conducted electronically, this system of voting harkened back to an older era whereby each member was called upon one by one, alphabetically, to stand and announce their choice before the entire chamber

"Adams?"

"Jeffries"

"Aderholt?"

"McCarthy"

And on and on until Ryan Zinke of Montana, taking roughly an hour in total for each round and slowly providing fodder for must-watch TV. Unfortunately for us, most of our problem children came early in the alphabet, leaving us officially deadlocked with six no votes before we even got to the letter "D."

Though not at all unexpected after that morning's tumultuous events, it was still a gut punch to actually hear those first few defections out loud—recalling how we felt when the Never Kevins began to spring up during the fall. Each defection was also accompanied by its own wave of gasps and murmurings across the House floor.

Even so, there was some relief in finally ripping off the Band-Aid.

Okay, that happened. I told myself. *But we're still in this. Let's keep plugging.*

Or, as Kevin would often say, "Just keep dancing."

By the end of the first ballot, the total was Jeffries 212, McCarthy 203, with 19 Freedom Caucus Republicans having scattered their votes between Biggs (10), Jordan (6), Jim Banks of Indiana (1), Lee Zeldin of New York (1), and Byron Donalds of Florida (1).

With no member surpassing the necessary 50 percent threshold, the Clerk of the House and presiding officer, Cheryl L. Johnson, then uttered a sentence that had not been heard in the House Chamber since before World War II: "No persons having received a majority of the whole number of votes cast by surname, a Speaker has not been elected."

* * *

As decided during our conversation with Vin Weber, step two in our plan was always to ask Jim Jordan to give Kevin's nominating speech before the second ballot. But we had not officially made that ask of Jim until right then and there on the floor.

"Jim, I'd like you to nominate me," Kevin asked.

"Whatever you need, Kevin," he replied without hesitation.

Jim furiously began scribbling down talking points—one, two, three. More so than most any other member in our conference, Jim Jordan possessed an innate ability to distill an argument down into its essentials; mini-sermons, almost, delivered in plainspoken language like "Do what we said we would do" that our Republican base ate up.

"For what purpose does the gentleman from Ohio seek recognition?" the Clerk of the House inquired.

"To rise to nominate Kevin McCarthy for Speaker of the House," Jim said, triggering an extended standing ovation on our side of the aisle.

"I think we have three objectives this Congress, three fundamental things we have to get done in the 118th Congress," he began.

"First, pass the bills that fix the problems," he said, ticking through a litany of President Biden's failures from the border and the military to energy, education policy, and the economy.

"Second, we can never ever let a bill like the one that passed twelve days ago—$1.7 trillion spent—we can never ever let that kind of legislation pass again," he added, referring to the omnibus government spending bill that Democrats had enacted on their way out the door a few weeks prior, further enraging our right flank.

"And then finally, third, we have to do the oversight and the investigations that need to be done."

He then turned to his and Kevin's personal journey, from being elected in the same class to running against each other to now fighting together on one team.

"I remember Kevin told me: 'The toughest times in life are when you get knocked down. The question is: Can you come back?' And I've always seen him be able to do that," he said.

"I hope you'll vote for Kevin McCarthy, and that's why I'm proud to nominate him for Speaker of the House," he concluded, prompting another loud ovation among the Republicans that ended with him and Kevin shaking hands and taking their seats.

While Jordan's speech had certainly left an impression on the Republican side of the aisle, Democrats also took notice and sought to stir the pot, suggesting that the real aim of the Freedom Caucus was to block Kevin so as to elevate Jim Jordan into the Speaker's chair.

"For half of that, I wasn't quite sure who the gentleman from Ohio was nominating," Democratic Caucus Chair Pete Aguilar quipped during his rebuttal nomination speech.

Our fears were only further fueled by the next member to rise for the purposes of a nomination, Matt Gaetz of Florida.

"Well, sometimes we have to do jobs that we don't really want to do, and sometimes we have to do jobs that we are called to do," Gaetz began. "And so, my colleagues, I rise to nominate the most talented, hardest working member of the Republican conference who just gave a speech with more vision than we have ever heard from the alternative. I'm nominating Jim Jordan."

Gaetz's speech prompted a flurry of text exchanges between our staff.

"Their intention is to have more come out for Jordan and it to pick up on the outside," Natalie Joyce suggested. "This is the play."

Sure enough, on the second ballot, the vote count was 212 for Jeffries, 203 for McCarthy, with all 19 HFC defections going to Jordan.

A potential alternative was brewing—and a potent one at that.

* * *

Ballot three tracked the same as the prior ballot until a surprise defection popped up—Byron Donalds of Florida.

As mentioned in chapter 9, Donalds had run for the position of conference chair earlier in the fall—garnering a surprisingly strong seventy-four votes in an ultimately unsuccessful challenge to incumbent Elise Stefanik—with much of his support coming from the Freedom Caucus.

Despite the loss, Donalds was clearly someone with his sights set on something greater. Only a sophomore, he already boasted one of the larger media footprints of any elected Republican, understanding that exposure was the new coin of the realm in a postmodern Washington.

"The reality is Rep. Kevin McCarthy doesn't have the votes," Donalds tweeted later that day, predictably triggering a swarm of media attention from the Hill and national press corps. "These continuous votes aren't working for anyone."

Even though it was just one vote, Donalds's defection meant that our count was officially trending in the wrong direction at the end of the third and final ballot of the day.

* * *

Stuck in the mud and now losing ground, our team regrouped back in the office and attempted to chart a path forward.

"I think we do a Five Families meeting without Kevin next," Natalie Joyce texted our group. "Gaetz told Graves that they would be amenable to changing names for committees—they mostly care about [Appropriations] and Rules."

Graves referred to Garret Graves of Louisiana—the most pleasant surprise of the week that helped make up for the sudden defection of Byron Donalds.

A former congressional staffer with boundless energy and a wicked sense of humor, Garret was originally brought into our orbit as Kevin's pick to serve as the top Republican on the Select Committee on Climate Change that was created by Democrats in 2019.

Even though Garret thrived in the role, I would not say I considered him and Kevin to be particularly close prior to that week in January 2023. In fact, he would have had every right to tell us to pound sand after Kevin opted against renewing the climate panel in the new Congress, in effect denying Garret a promotion to chairman.

Rather than take his ball and go home, however, Garret saw a void and stepped into the fray that week without ever being asked to help. He took it upon himself to begin talking with as many of the twenty holdouts as he could, trying to parse through those who just wanted to spite Kevin and those who actually were interested in finding common ground to form a governing coalition. For added effect, he continued to grow out his lengthy salt-and-pepper beard that dated back to no-shave November, refusing to trim it until Kevin was elected Speaker.

While everyone agreed that we needed to get a meeting on the books with the detractors and fast, we unfortunately found that many of them had already left campus and were now ducking our calls. Others spent the evening calling other Republicans to try to encourage further defections, spreading rumors that Kevin's vote count would get worse and worse with each successive ballot.

With Garret's help, we eventually managed to drag a few folks back to the Capitol to talk, including Chip Roy, Scott Perry, and Matt Gaetz. The three met in Majority Whip Tom Emmer's office along with a few of our hand-picked intermediaries including Chief Deputy Whip Guy Reschenthaler of Pennsylvania, French Hill and Bruce Westerman of Arkansas, Tom Cole of Oklahoma, and Kelly Armstrong of North Dakota. From where we sat, it was better to have others speak on our behalf so as to avoid the personality-driven conflicts that continued to fester between the HFC and Kevin.

For his part, Gaetz repeatedly stated that his only purpose in being there was to relay the fact that Kevin would never get the necessary votes and that he believed it was time for the conference to go "post-McCarthy."

"Why are we even having this conversation?" Gaetz repeatedly questioned.

Majority Whip Emmer strongly pushed back, however, and said Kevin was the nominee and that the group would only be discussing ways to elevate him to Speaker. When it became apparent to Gaetz that everyone in the room shared the whip's position and had no interest in entertaining plans to abandon Kevin, Gaetz angrily excused himself from the meeting.

While Scott Perry seemed to gravitate toward Gaetz's new "post-McCarthy" mantra—potentially as a means to get himself off the hook for having to negotiate a truce—he largely stayed quiet. Meanwhile, Chip spoke about throwing a Hail Mary to revive some talks around the original agreement that had been under discussion, including appointments of Freedom Caucus members to the Rules Committee, a return of the one-person Motion to Vacate, and clearer targets on federal spending that would be pursued by our conference.

So you're saying there's a chance I thought to myself as notes of the meeting were relayed to us afterward by our allies.

Nevertheless, the meeting adjourned without any firm resolution or steps forward. To make matters worse, several of our allies left the meeting feeling more than a little spooked, unsure if the hardcore Never Kevins would ever break and fretting that others might soon follow the path of Byron Donalds and defect publicly.

Internally, Kevin summed up the stalemate to everyone as analogous to a government shutdown.

"Off the bat, both sides are excited and think they are winning," he said. "It's only after a few days does one side realize they're losing and tries to look for an off-ramp."

The analogy seemed appropriate. At the end of day one, we were firmly at the stage in the fight where both sides had convinced themselves that they had the upper hand and would prevail in the end if they only held out long enough.

From the point of view of the Freedom Caucus, they left the Capitol riding high after having held together for three straight votes, forcing the first multi-ballot Speaker's contest in a century, and picking up a surprise defection along the way. This was no small feat.

Meanwhile, we felt good that we had held the two hundred, over 90 percent of the conference. Likewise, thanks to the work of Matt Sparks and our communications team, Kevin received largely positive air cover that night on television with both Laura Ingraham and Sean Hannity making the case on Fox that a protracted fight only served to empower Democrats and President Biden—a crucial element that we were lacking in the 2015 run for Speaker.

Indeed, the fight had begun. It was occurring on the House floor, it was occurring behind closed doors, it was occurring in the public square, and it was occurring on the airwaves.

But as they say, "No plan survives first contact with the enemy." And only time would tell whose plan would win out.

CHAPTER 15

JANUARY 4, 2023—LAST WILL AND TESTAMENT

The next morning, I woke up in a cold sweat at around 5 a.m.

"It feels like the walls are closing in," I texted former coworker Ben Howard.

How are we going to get these guys to break, I asked myself, *if they're barely even talking to us?*

To the outside world, we did our best to keep up the appearance of "active negotiations." But if the hastily organized and inconclusive meeting from the night before was any indication, the reality was far bleaker. Now fully co-opted by Matt Gaetz, the Freedom Caucus was more bought in than ever around his plan to continue voting for someone other than Kevin until the conference eventually and inevitably exhausted itself.

Apparently Kevin harbored similar feelings that morning as he broached the subject for the very first time aloud of what ought to happen if he could not secure the votes needed.

"You always need to have a will in place," he told the small group of our senior staff huddled in his office.

Several of us tried to cut the conversation off, but Kevin was insistent that we discuss who could—and, more importantly—who *should* be the Speaker of the House if it was not meant to be for him.

Majority Leader Steve Scalise and Majority Whip Tom Emmer's names were discussed, though Scalise had been conspicuously absent from the attempts at talks over the past twenty-four hours. Committee chairs like Financial Services Chair Patrick McHenry, Judiciary Chair Jim Jordan, Rules Committee Chair Tom Cole, and Natural Resources Chair Bruce Westerman were also raised, as was quickly budding rock star Garret Graves.

Although the conversation did not last more than ten or fifteen minutes and did not settle on any one clear choice, it had the effect of injecting a sense of urgency into us at the staff level. Not only were we fighting a restless conference, but we now had to be sure that our ever-optimistic boss did not lose his will to fight either.

* * *

That is not to say the morning was all doom and gloom. Instead, we awoke to a positive statement of support from former President Trump, who Kevin had remained close with and who continued to carry outsized influence within the party following his first term.

"It's now time for all of our GREAT Republican House Members to VOTE FOR KEVIN, CLOSE THE DEAL, TAKE THE VICTORY," it began (emphasis, of course, his).

"DO NOT TURN A GREAT TRIUMPH INTO A GIANT & EMBARRASSING DEFEAT. IT'S TIME TO CELEBRATE, YOU DESERVE IT. Kevin McCarthy will do a good job, and maybe even a GREAT JOB—JUST WATCH!" the statement concluded.

Nevertheless, even this full-throated pronouncement did not immediately loosen any votes from the Freedom Caucus bloc as we rapidly approached our noon reconvening time on January 4.

As previously mentioned, since this was all happening at the beginning of a new Congress, there were not yet any official House rules in place, such as the typical authority for the Speaker to declare a recess. That power would have been particularly handy right about then, allowing us to dictate the pace of when and how votes would occur.

Unfortunately, absent these standing rules, we were at the mercy of whatever 218 members would agree to at any given moment. And while the Democrats were willing to go along the day before in consenting to a recess to protect their many opening-night soirees, we would find no such luck heading into day two of the stalemate. Instead, my Democratic counterparts made clear that their members were prepared to oppose any move to adjourn and would force us to pass such a motion with 218 votes on our side.

Further complicating matters, we found ourselves battling sudden attendance challenges from two Texas representatives: Roger Williams and Wesley Hunt.

Williams's wife, Patty, had recently experienced a medical emergency, and he was understandably grief-stricken, longing to be at her side for her series of doctor's appointments over the coming days. We told him that it would probably be at least another day or two before we would be in any sort of position to bridge the gap with the holdouts and advised him to go be with his wife until we could signal a breakthrough.

With tears in his eyes, he relayed to us that Patty told him, "it's more important for you to be there and voting for Kevin. Stay."

If that doesn't give you goose bumps, I don't know what will.

Meanwhile, freshman Wesley Hunt was eager to be with his family, too, as his wife cared for their newborn child who had been born several weeks premature, such that both baby and mother were going back and forth from the NICU in Houston.

It was impossible to argue with either of their circumstances, and we did not try to. But without the Texans present and voting for Kevin, it was also all but impossible that we could cobble together a winning majority.

* * *

With no other choice, we readied ourselves to endure another round of balloting at noon.

Mike Gallagher of Wisconsin, who Kevin had tapped that fall to be the chair of his newly created bipartisan Select Committee on China, volunteered himself to give a nominating speech. He shared a few excerpts from his prepared remarks with our team the night before, and we all agreed that they were pitch perfect to reset the tone and put a positive spin on the situation.

"So here we are. It's January 4th. Start of a new Congress, and we're all supposed to be taking pictures with our families in Statuary Hall," Gallagher began. "Instead we're here in the chamber. And you know what? There's nowhere I'd rather be."

"Sure it looks messy, but democracy is messy by design. We make our mistakes out in the open for all to see. We air our disagreements in front of the American people, for whom we work," he continued. "That's a feature, not a bug of our system."

Never underestimate the importance of controlling the narrative. We always found it was better to give members something positive to say than let them freelance on their own. And while it would have been easy to describe the current situation as a debacle, Gallagher's remarks successfully helped our allies reframe the back-and-forth playing out between Kevin and the Freedom Caucus as simply the latest episode in America's turbulent yet ultimately resilient experiment of self-governance.

In response, my friend Chip Roy spoke on behalf of the Freedom Caucus and nominated Byron Donalds of Florida as their pick for Speaker, the surprise flip from the day before.

This shift to Donalds from Jim Jordan was the second welcome development of the day and one of the key turning points of the week. With Jordan's massive name identification and increasing credibility inside our conference, a sustained effort of voting for Jordan could have spurred an outpouring of support from the grassroots and shaken the faith of our allies. After all, the goal was still to "never let an alternative emerge."

By all accounts, however, Jim begged off such a move, telling his colleagues in the Freedom Caucus that he did not want their votes and that they should instead back Kevin.

That led the HFC to search for a new champion—their third in two days after Biggs and Jordan—which they found in the sophomore from Naples.

While Donalds was not able to build upon the twenty votes that Jordan had received the day prior, a lengthy conversation with Freedom Caucus Chair Scott Perry resulted in Indiana Representative Victoria Spartz switching her vote from McCarthy to "present," a change that she justified in the press as an attempt to initiate further discussions among the conference on the path forward.

"I think it's important for us as Republicans to address concern[s] and come to an agreement and not waste everyone's time—and we need to have further deliberation to make sure that we can elect a Speaker," Spartz told CNN later that day. "We need to go back to the conference room and have this discussion, not wasting time [sic] on the floor because no one is going to budge."

We continued to pick up rumblings of other members who might be getting shaky, perhaps eager to earn some free media coverage for themselves, as well.

"There are a few of those twenty that just aren't going to vote for Kevin McCarthy but would vote for somebody else," Ken Buck of Colorado told the press that day.

"I said to Kevin, at some point, you know, you've got to make sure you gotta either cut a deal or you've got to give Steve [Scalise] a chance or others a chance to see if they can put it together," Buck added, all but confirming that he was not someone who could be counted on for the long haul.

* * *

After the fourth ballot, I tried to catch my breath for a few minutes in the back of the chamber. That is, until Patrick McHenry found me.

"What is the plan? Get your game face on," he barked. "You look like your dog died. Snap out of it."

Frankly, I would not have disputed his characterization. Following over fifty days of nonstop work since the midterm elections, the stress of the race was really beginning to take its toll on all of us. Some staff resorted to Ambien to try to get a decent night's sleep. Many had fallen physically ill over the holidays and were still recovering. Afrin was used well beyond the recommended three days. Meanwhile, I more or less completely lost my appetite, sustaining myself on smoothies that my wife and close friends would deliver to the Republican cloakroom at the start of each day's votes. By the end of the week, I had lost ten pounds, making me even lankier than usual.

Kevin also shared that he was losing around a pound a day dating back to the winter.

"The best diet I've ever had is running for Speaker!" he would joke.

McHenry, however, was in no mood for jokes.

"Where are the meetings? What are we doing to get people talking?" he demanded.

Unlike the night before, he stressed that we move quickly so as to not let any holdouts leave the Capitol building. If we kept them inside the building, he reasoned, they would not be able to be on TV trashing us or alone with each other further conspiring against us.

Member Services Director Natalie Joyce was receiving similar feedback.

"Members are feeling the whip effort feels lacking in both strategy and tactics," she texted. "They don't feel like we have a plan."

In haste, we began to write down a list of Freedom Caucus members on a sheet of paper who were gettable and divvied them up based on what issues they cared about. On the other side of the paper, we wrote down the best allies who could address those concerns while feverishly typing up a black letter proposal that these allies could study and use to negotiate with on our behalf inside the meetings.

* * *

As Warren Davidson of Ohio took the podium to nominate Kevin ahead of the fifth ballot, we pitched our idea of holding two medium-size meetings to the Freedom Caucus. They indicated they were open to the idea but wanted to continue balloting in the meantime.

Prior to that week, we had not anticipated needing so many members to give nominating speeches, so finding the right individual proved to be a persistent assignment. Thankfully, Davidson—a member of the Freedom Caucus—knocked it out of the park, directly appealing to his fellow conservatives from their point of view and ticking through the litany of places where Kevin had found common ground with them to make the institution run in a more open and fair way.

"I feel at this time, we risk a worse outcome if we cannot unite behind the man who has helped us achieve these substantive reforms. Reforms that offer all of us—this whole body—hope for change to the broken status quo. Reforms our voters demand and reforms we have worked hard together to achieve," he stated.

Chip Roy's team called it the best speech so far. Likewise, Tim Reitz of the Freedom Caucus asked for a copy so he could send the list of reforms that Davidson referenced to all the members of the caucus, such as ending the practice of "voting by proxy" that Democrats had created during the pandemic.

Whether it was our offer to meet, Davidson's speech, or something else entirely, the widespread predictions of a swelling opposition failed to materialize on the fifth and sixth ballots. Instead, both tallies mirrored the fourth ballot exactly: Jeffries 212, McCarthy 201, and Donalds of Florida 20, with one answering present.

Despite the detractors' best efforts, we were still standing.

* * *

Having reached an apparent stalemate, I approached Matt Gaetz after the sixth ballot to float the idea of an adjournment. With the Democrats already having told us that they would not vote for any breaks in the action, we had no other choice but to try to put together 218 Republicans on our own, which unfortunately included Mr. Gaetz.

"Cards on the table, I love seeing the chyron that says 'McCarthy losing support,'" Gaetz exclaimed to me.

"I get that. And I think you've achieved that," I replied. "But what are we going to do next is the question?"

By that point, a group of members had gathered around me and him at the leadership desk in the center of the floor. While Gaetz remained as animated and defiant as ever, it also seemed like he was unsure of what his next move ought to be. After all, if Kevin continued to hold back the tide, the pressure would only be amplified on the Never Kevins to produce a valid justification for the stalemate. Perhaps a break would be to his benefit, as well, to search for more targets to add to the defections list that he so relished.

While he and I were briefly in agreement on adjourning until the next day at noon, Majority Leader Steve Scalise entered our conversation after a few minutes and suggested reconvening at 8 p.m. that day. Gaetz quickly jumped at Scalise's idea and agreed to allow for the much shorter recess than we had been discussing.

* * *

While any break was better than no break, an 8 p.m. restart time gave us only a few hours to hold additional talks. And as if things weren't complicated enough, even the question of where the meeting would be held became contentious.

Earlier in the week, Matt Gaetz accused Kevin of "squatting" in the Speaker's office and refused to enter the suite so long as Kevin and our staff remained in it. That took our office off the table.

We inquired about using the conference room in Majority Leader Scalise's office one floor above ours, but his team claimed that it was already booked for that evening—the latest peculiarity from their team given that no other business was set to occur until a Speaker was elected.

Thankfully, Majority Whip Tom Emmer volunteered his offices on the first floor, H-107, the same ones where I first began my work with Kevin as a college intern. I had certainly come a long way from those days of restocking shelves and making copies to now being one of the central staffers in this unfolding drama. And for the remainder of the week, the first home base I ever knew in the Capitol would become our central meeting place for the peace talks.

We ultimately settled on two medium-size meetings with holdouts and allies divided along issue sets. Group one included McCarthy, McHenry, Graves, Kelly Armstrong of North Dakota, Tom Cole of Oklahoma, and Brian Fitzpatrick of Pennsylvania alongside Jim Jordan, Scott Perry, Chip Roy, Byron Donalds, Andy Harris of Maryland, and Andrew Clyde of Georgia with the focus being on House rules and our legislative agenda.

Group two included Majority Whip Emmer, Chief Deputy Whip Guy Reschenthaler, Richard Hudson of North Carolina, Dusty Johnson of South Dakota, Jason Smith of Missouri, and Bruce Westerman of Arkansas opposite Lauren Boebert, Dan Bishop of North Carolina, Michael Cloud of Texas, Paul Gosar of Arizona, Anna Paulina Luna of Florida, and Josh Brecheen of Oklahoma with the focus being appropriations and spending.

Gaetz, meanwhile, was intentionally left off the list. Despite not being an official member of the Freedom Caucus, he had essentially become their leader that week, commandeering the twenty holdouts to wage his personal crusade against Kevin. We determined that keeping him away was our best and only shot to whittle down the opposition—a "cancer that needs to be extracted," as I described him to Patrick McHenry.

Nevertheless, just as we were about to begin our meeting, who barged into the room but Matt Gaetz. The press reported seeing him scrambling around the Capitol, frantically asking where the members were meeting. From where I was sitting, it almost felt as though he kicked open the door, the crashing sound startling everyone in the room.

"What's going on here?" he shouted.

Chip Roy and Scott Perry both looked up at him sheepishly, like two kids caught with their hand in the cookie jar.

"We're . . . just talking," Perry nervously answered.

"Talking about what? He's never going to be Speaker!" Gaetz shouted again.

After some uncomfortable glances were shared across the room, Gaetz tried to get Ralph Norman to leave with him.

"We don't need this—right, Ralph?"

But the group gently encouraged Norman to take a seat and stay. When given the chance, my experience was that members usually preferred to be in the room where it happened. That is what Norman chose, further sending Gaetz into a tizzy.

"Well, I'm never voting for you!" he screamed, slamming Emmer's door on his way out.

Down the hall, Gaetz tried to pull the same stunt with group two in the conference room. After lingering for a bit, he staged an almost identical blowup.

"We don't need to hear this, right guys?" he boomed, expecting to incite a dramatic walkout.

This time, it was Josh Brecheen, a mild-mannered yet serious freshman from Oklahoma, who mustered up the courage to respond.

"Well, I'd like to hear what they have to say," he said.

Another freshman, Anna Paulina Luna, agreed. "Me too."

Maybe we have an opening here? It was the first glimmer of hope I had felt in quite a while.

* * *

Back in Emmer's quarters, Kevin tried to bring the temperatures down.

"Listen, my intention was not for conference to go how it did," he began, referencing the morning meeting from the day prior. "Tensions were high, and that set us back. But you've always heard me say that we should not act on emotion."

He turned the conversation toward the idea of expanding the Elected Leadership Committee or ELC table to include members of each of the Five Families at the high-level weekly strategy sessions hosted in the Speaker's office. Previously, only elected members of leadership were included, but invitations were fully at the discretion of the Speaker.

What came next was a stroke of genius. Kevin looked directly at Byron Donalds and proposed that he serve as both the Freedom Caucus designee at the leadership table as well as Kevin's personal pick on the exclusive Steering Committee tasked with doling out committee assignments.

Choosing Donalds for either of these slots had not previously occurred to me, but Kevin was two steps ahead as usual. He knew that Donalds harbored higher aspirations and was now dangling in front of him the one thing that any ambitious member coveted: a new title. Even better, this one came without the trouble of having to run and win a leadership race.

"Byron, you get how the Freedom Caucus thinks, but you also work well with the rest of the conference. You would be perfect for the room," Kevin told him, leaning forward and looking him directly in the eyes.

Jordan nodded, as did Perry and Roy. Donalds cracked a wry smile, lapping up the praise he was receiving and agreeing that he was indeed a "unique bridge" inside the conference.

As an added bonus, this move would simultaneously block the Freedom Caucus' preferred pick for Steering—Dan Bishop of North Carolina—from gaining entrance into the inner sanctum of House Republican politics.

Most crucial for our purposes, however, was from that point forward, Donalds supplanted Gaetz as the Freedom Caucus' de facto leader in the negotiations. Whereas Scott Perry and Chip Roy had thus far failed at rallying the troops on their own, Donalds now assumed the mantle of HFC point man, driven by the very real incentive of knowing that he was unlikely to get any better offer for himself than the one Kevin just presented. In fact, Garret Graves cornered Donalds at the end of the meeting to drive home that very point.

"Byron, you need to flip for Kevin. Nobody got more than you in that meeting and you know it," he insisted. "Now, we need to show progress."

Donalds seemed to acknowledge Graves's point, but he did not outright commit to flipping—at least not yet.

* * *

Walking to the floor for the 8 p.m. restart time, the Freedom Caucus had told us they were good to adjourn until the following day so they could discuss all of the day's developments with their members overnight and into the morning.

"All I can tell you is that we had a productive meeting," Scott Perry told the press on his way out of Majority Whip Emmer's office.

Even so, the vote to adjourn was anything but easy. In fact, the motion was failing at one point, with four Republicans voting no—Andy Biggs, Lauren Boebert, Eli Crane, and Matt Gaetz.

I was in the cloakroom going over my notes with Tim Reitz from the Freedom Caucus when we both looked up at a nearby TV monitor and saw the vote in danger of going down. We ran out to the floor and I urged him to get his guys to go in as a yes, while Democrats angrily shouted at the Clerk of the House to close the vote.

In the end, two Democrats missed the vote, allowing us to barely squeak by and adjourn amid a chaotic scene of yelling by members on both sides. Had those Democrats been present, the motion would have failed. Later, Arizona Representative Andy Biggs claimed that allowing us to adjourn that night was the Never Kevins' biggest strategic blunder, giving us more time and oxygen to make continued progress.

Conversely, I celebrated with our members and staff at the leadership desk.

"We're becoming a majority!" I exclaimed, only half tongue-in-cheek. It was the first recorded vote we had actually won in the new Congress and perhaps one of the hardest-fought adjournment votes in history. More importantly, it was a further sign that Gaetz was losing his grip on the Freedom Caucus and that they were splintering.

"I felt as though we had a very good discussion," Kevin told the press that evening. "I think what you should gauge is, being able to do that [adjournment] vote, is that the discussions are going well and they're continuing."

* * *

We followed our win on the floor with an equally important victory off the floor as our main Super PAC, the Congressional Leadership Fund (CLF), brokered a deal with the Club for Growth—one of the leading outside conservative organizations and frequent thorns in our side—on establishing parameters around when and where the PAC would be allowed to engage in Republican primaries.

"CLF will not spend in any open-seat primaries in safe Republican districts and CLF will not grant resources to other super PACs to do so," CLF executive director Dan Conston said in a joint statement with the Club, addressing an issue that had persistently come up on the Freedom Caucus' list of grievances.

"This agreement on super PACs fulfills a major concern we have pressed for," Club for Growth President David McIntosh added. "We understand that Leader McCarthy and Members are working on a rules agreement that will meet the principles we have set out previously."

"Assuming these principles are met," McIntosh continued, "Club for Growth will support Kevin McCarthy for Speaker."

In reality, the agreement did not neuter CLF's ability to intervene in primaries where necessary, as the PAC could still make use of difficult-to-track shell organizations to funnel resources to our preferred candidates. Even so, holdout Dan Bishop of North Carolina later described what the apparent truce with Club for Growth meant at that moment in time with regard to the momentum the Freedom Caucus was feeling just a day prior.

"It undermined our negotiating posture," Bishop said. "It really, sort of, cut our legs out from under us Wednesday evening."

"It just came at us. None of us were alerted to it ahead of time. It was a surprise to us," he continued. "And for people to go out saying that something substantial had been resolved when we're in here, kind of fighting it out over getting things—it was not helpful."

Ironically, the person I bumped into on my walk back home to the Navy Yard that night was none other than Dan Bishop.

"So what do you think?" I asked him as we stood underneath a streetlight on Independence Avenue outside the Longworth House Office Building.

"There's promise," he smiled and said to me.

Compared to that morning when I walked in the Capitol and our first conversation was about getting a last will and testament in order, promise was more than enough for me.

CHAPTER 16

JANUARY 5, 2023—MEMBER MANAGEMENT

We awoke on the morning of January 5 to an urgent text from Dusty Johnson of South Dakota.

"We have a rebellion in Main Street," he said, referring to the more establishment-leaning Republican caucus of which he was the cochair. "We have to have someone come tell the group whatever little bit can be told. If we don't let a little pressure out of this container, people are going to start to say and do unhelpful things."

The sentiment was not necessarily a surprise. We were under immense pressure to provide an update to the scores of antsy members who understandably felt as though they were being left in the dark. The irony was not lost on anyone that for as much as the Freedom Caucus decried "swampy backroom dealings behind closed doors," here they were doing that very thing.

Adding to the pressure, Scalise allies began soliciting signatures on a draft petition to call for a special conference meeting, which would have been a legitimate powder keg. We caught wind of the movement early and Kevin and some of the leaders of the petition were able to connect, agreeing to schedule a member-wide conference call instead. But the clock was now officially ticking.

* * *

Hoping to head off this very scenario, we drafted a letter the night prior to provide an update for the conference. At the last minute, though, we were begged off from sending it by Tim Reitz of the Freedom Caucus who feared that doing so would only make his guys feel as though they were being boxed in. This proved to be the constant push and pull all week, and our team was none too pleased.

"He needs to know the other side is getting agitated about not being involved in conversations, and we have to update them soon," Natalie Joyce commented.

"Makes it harder for us with moderates," Dan Meyer added. "I would hope they'd understand that."

Meanwhile, Matt Gaetz was busy stoking the flames by leaking misinformation about the emerging agreement in the hopes of derailing it in its tracks, including an absurd rumor that Chip Roy was going to replace Tom Cole as Chair of the Rules Committee. Unfortunately, his efforts seemed to be working.

"Confidences betrayed do not inspire trust," Freedom Caucus Chair Scott Perry told the press that morning in response to being asked about the leaks.

Fortunately, a Capitol Hill reporter tweeted out that his source for information was none other than Gaetz, which I promptly forwarded to Tim and the other Freedom Caucus members with whom I was in regular communication.

"Here is your leak," I said. "It's not us. It's him trying to undo it all."

* * *

In the meantime, Kevin decided to make a surprise appearance at that morning's Main Street Caucus meeting. The room was completely packed, with members jammed shoulder to shoulder in a nondescript space across from the Members' Dining Room on the first floor of the Capitol.

To me, it felt like a throwback from a bygone era, one seen in black-and-white photographs of candidates giving speeches off the back of a train car. There was no social media here. No cookie-cutter remarks, choreographed camera ops, or staff-provided voting recommendations. This was person-to-person, raw, retail politics.

Fittingly, Kevin spoke off the cuff.

"I know everyone wants information," he began. "I would like to give you that information, but the challenge is that we cannot control when we adjourn."

"The only change to the rules package we released over the weekend is one number—changing the Motion to Vacate from five people to one person," he said, touching upon the most-discussed rules change. "That's not something you love or I love, but it's also not something that I fear."

He then gave them his pitch on how we would need to start thinking differently this Congress. With the margins as they stood, any five members could bring the House to a screeching halt at any point—Motion to Vacate or not. Thus, we better all figure out how to get along quickly or else nothing would be able to get done.

"I also plan to expand the elected leadership table. Yes, adding a Freedom Caucus member, but also adding someone from your group, as well as from the RSC, Tuesday Group, and Problem Solvers," he continued, enabling him to do for the rest of the Five Families what he did for Donalds the day before.

Finally, he concluded by emphasizing what he felt was at stake in the current fight and why he was in it for the long haul.

"Listen, I know some of you may not love me. You may have friends who you would rather see be Speaker," he said, while I scanned the room to gauge the reaction of potential fence-sitters.

"But this isn't about me anymore," he added. "This is about our conference and our country."

Members began to nod and applaud.

"If we give in now, this will happen every single time. Is that what you want?"

"No!" the room roared back.

"Good. So I am not backing down," he stated. "I will never give up and I will never, ever forget all of you for standing with me. Thank you."

With that, the room erupted in a standing ovation. Members patted Kevin on the back and shook his hand as he walked down the center aisle. His speech had done the trick and quelled the rank-and-file rebellion—at least for now.

* * *

Despite the prior day's progress, it was unclear if we were going to be able to show any positive movement on the floor in terms of votes heading into the third day of balloting.

Instead, we were made aware of another unexpected absence as Representative Ken Buck—who had voiced skepticism of Kevin's bid the day before—departed Washington without any advance warning for a planned non-emergency medical procedure back in Colorado.

To keep the conversations going, we adopted a 4x4 framework that our chief Dan Meyer had proposed, with Roy, Bishop, Perry, and Donalds serving on behalf of the Freedom Caucus and Tom Emmer, Garret Graves, French Hill of Arkansas, and Brian Fitzpatrick of Pennsylvania speaking for us.

You could not have asked for a stronger team to represent our interests. Between Emmer, the unflappable Midwestern whip; Graves, the tenacious Cajun confidant; Hill, the meticulous Southern gentleman; and Fitzpatrick, the centrist Northeastern dealmaker—it was a genuine dream team.

The group met in Whip Emmer's conference room throughout the day for a lively series of meetings, breaking only when a member would need to run up to the floor to cast their vote. For good measure, Patrick McHenry was called in at a crucial impasse to shed light on the Steering process, where he proceeded to unleash a string of expletives on the recalcitrant Freedom Caucus members when he learned they were demanding a quota for their members on both Steering and several key standing committees.

"No fucking way," McHenry responded. "Fuck you. Fuck you. Fuck you!"

By that point, the race had become borderline must-see TV. People who otherwise knew little about politics were captivated by the old-fashioned process playing out before their eyes and drawn into the drama of a political endurance test rarely seen in the modern era. In total, we survived five ballots that day, the most of any day so far.

Sitting on the floor, Kevin and I would seesaw off one another. Anytime I would start to get down, he would buck me up and vice versa. We also utilized the Speaker's ceremonial office off the back of the House floor as a greenroom of sorts, rolling in two large television screens for live viewing along with a constant parade of Kevin's friends and allies to keep spirits high. The mental challenge of spending so much time with detractors was a real one and simply having Kevin be surrounded by friendly faces and encouraging words was a huge morale boost in between ballots.

Throughout, my phone was abuzz with texts from family and friends telling us to keep up the good fight and not let Gaetz and his crew win.

Even a colleague who worked on the whip floor team of Democratic Congressman Jim Clyburn told me one day in the hallway: "You'll get there. Don't worry."

To return to the shutdown analogy, we felt that the public was strongly on our side and assumed that sentiment was being felt by the holdouts, as well.

Gaetz's erratic behavior seemed to validate our opinion, with him voting for Donald Trump for Speaker on the first two ballots of the day. Whether that was a Hail Mary attempt to engage the grassroots or simply fodder for his constant stream of fundraising emails, it seemed as though he and the Never Kevins were increasingly grasping at straws.

Nevertheless, pockets of interesting conversations continued to bubble up on and around the floor. We stumbled upon Representative Jodey Arrington whispering with a fellow Texan in the cloakroom. It was later relayed that Arrington was quietly floating his own name for Speaker and attempting to leverage the powerful Texas delegation as his anchor.

Likewise, Steve Scalise's former Chief Deputy Whip Drew Ferguson of Georgia was seen engaged in a long conversation with Never Kevin Matt Rosendale of Montana—and I don't believe it was about convincing him to vote for us.

As the day went on, you could notice that certain members' previously confident voice votes for Kevin became softer and softer, and we knew that several of them were conspiring in private. To quote former Speaker Boehner: "You know who you are."

* * *

Beyond the rank and file, we also had our work cut out for us to keep the rest of our leadership team apprised and on board with what was happening with the Freedom Caucus.

For starters, the Rules Committee was agitated to learn that Kevin was willing to put multiple Freedom Caucus members on their panel. Likewise, Leader Scalise's team was upset that we had been discussing what bills might go on the floor, a function that was typically the purview of the majority leader. To address all the concerns head-on, we scheduled an impromptu meeting of the Elected Leadership Committee that evening.

From our end, we hoped the meeting would be a positive one, as the updates we were receiving from down in Emmer's office were that the group was closing in on a deal, perhaps as soon as that night. Instead, Kevin later admitted that this leadership meeting was one of the points where he truly felt that it was all going to fall apart—that trying to thread the needle between the asks of the Freedom Caucus and the needs of the center of the conference was going to be simply too difficult to achieve.

While members of the leadership team raised issues with the number of Rules Committee slots and the proposed bills to be considered, the real flash point was a discussion around spending targets that our lead policy staffer, Brittan Specht, had been hashing out downstairs.

As Brittan began to walk the team through what was being negotiated—namely, a return to the spending levels of 2022—longtime appropriator and chairman of the Rules Committee Tom Cole spoke up.

"That is simply not possible," he said, not mincing words.

Doing so would entail a major cut to defense spending, he explained, and an even bigger cut to nondefense spending—the largest pot of money that Cole himself had overseen in his role as the lead Republican on the appropriations health subcommittee.

Conference Chair Elise Stefanik of New York also chimed in and voiced her opposition to cutting defense spending, with her district being the home of Fort Drum and a large servicemember and veteran population. Others nodded along.

This is no bueno, I thought to myself.

Going into that meeting, we were hopeful that we could put the finishing touches on an agreement and perhaps even get 218 votes on the floor that night. But as the discussion with our bleary-eyed leadership team continued to devolve, Kevin quickly pivoted and asked me to find a way to get the House to adjourn—which we somehow managed to pull off yet again.

As members of the leadership team began to file out of the ceremonial office, Garret Graves and Patrick McHenry found Tom Cole and had a long chat with him on the now-empty House floor.

To his credit, Cole said that he was just doing what Kevin had asked for in the room: giving his honest opinion on what was being proposed. But he assured the two that he wanted Kevin to be Speaker and that whatever that entailed, he would support.

Tom Cole was the quintessential "old bull"—a member who had seen it all before, was not fazed by anything, and did not take shit from anyone. In fact, as a sign of respect, I once gifted Cole a framed picture of an old bull African water buffalo that I photographed on safari—with an accompanying bottle of Buffalo Trace bourbon for good measure.

At the same time, old bulls also respected the chain of command, viewing it as a bedrock foundation of how Congress got things done—along with other time-honored traditions like settling differences late into the night over cigars and a drink that are sadly at risk of going extinct like their namesakes who still practice them.

Through it all, I maintained the utmost admiration for our Rules chairman. He was a loyal soldier in the best sense of the word—and his continued support signaled that we remained on the right path.

* * *

Back in the office, a completely different problem was unfolding as Representative Marjorie Taylor Greene was trying to talk Kevin into going on Tucker Carlson's prime-time Fox program that evening with Matt Gaetz, ostensibly to negotiate a truce live on air.

While that would have certainly made for great television, those of us who were there in 2015 immediately had nightmare flashbacks to the Hannity incident that derailed Kevin's first bid. Needless to say, none of us were eager to see history repeat itself.

Though most of the major Fox personalities were behind us this time around, Tucker was a complete wild card and hunted elected officials for sport. In particular, he saved his sharpest criticisms for Republicans. After all, anyone could attack Democrats—but attacking Republicans was the real way to make a name for yourself with the base, both in the halls of Congress and in the conservative media ecosystem.

From where I sat, going on Tucker's program was a risky gambit in the best of times. Doing so now under duress—joined by Matt Gaetz, no less—was downright suicidal.

Thankfully, the idea never truly got off the ground, and Kevin opted to call Tucker instead to give him an update on where things stood between him and the Freedom Caucus.

"I think I am gonna win this," Kevin told Tucker. "I wanted to go tonight but we had a few attendance issues. But I think this will be over tomorrow."

"Really?" Tucker replied in his trademark quizzical tone, not betraying any emotion one way or another. "Wow, well, that would certainly be big news. Thank you for sharing that with me. I appreciate it."

Another bullet dodged.

* * *

Down in Majority Whip Emmer's office, the final contours of an agreement were being ironed out. The Freedom Caucus would have two members placed on the Rules Committee to be chosen by Kevin, not the four slots originally sought earlier in the week. In addition to these two slots, Kevin would appoint Thomas Massie of Kentucky to the committee, a member respected by everyone as a committed institutionalist and a neutral referee.

Theoretically, if Massie and the two Freedom Caucus picks voted with the four Democrats on the panel, it would be enough to block a bill from moving forward, which was the power the Freedom Caucus truly coveted.

Though some pundits described this as a major concession, we reasoned that if three Republicans were mad enough to vote no in committee, the rule would never pass the House anyway since only five Republicans were needed to tank a measure on the floor. From our vantage point, it was better to have a canary in the coal mine up at Rules and sniff out any issues rather than waste a day and learn the hard way. Plus, there was always the suspension calendar as a work-around for the must-pass bills that had broad bipartisan support.

In the end, Kevin landed on Chip Roy and Ralph Norman as his Freedom Caucus picks, which he balanced out by adding New York freshman Nick Langworthy and Indiana freshman Erin Houchin to the committee, two rising stars who represented the governing wing of the party.

Similarly, we pledged to work on increasing the number of Freedom Caucus members on certain standing committees where they felt they lacked representation, including the Appropriations Committee. While this certainly felt like a "diversity, equity, and inclusion" request from the HFC, we hoped that giving them a window into the nitty-gritty decision-making would help to demystify the process and open their eyes to the fact that leadership could not wave a magic wand and produce results. This also went for the Steering Committee, where Kevin upheld his commitment to appoint Byron Donalds as the "Speaker's appointee."

While the Freedom Caucus viewed these moves as wins for their group, Kevin also pushed the Steering Committee to add more members from each of the Five Families to "A Committees" across the board, including his appointment of multiple moderate members from the Northeast to the coveted Ways and Means Committee that handled tax policy. Once again, the goal was for each panel to better reflect the ideological makeup of our conference, thereby forcing members to work with one another in committee rather than deferring all the hard choices to the leadership team down the road.

A short list of bills that the Freedom Caucus wanted to see move through regular order was drawn up, including a strict border security bill that would end up becoming our H.R. 2—indicating the second-highest-priority measure of the Congress—as well as a bill proposing term limits for members of Congress. We pledged that these bills would receive consideration in their committee of jurisdiction, where they would need to sink or swim on their own merits—another commitment we upheld.

Finally, language was being workshopped on specific spending goals, with the new target being to reduce nondefense discretionary spending to 2022 levels. This shift to "nondefense discretionary" was important as it did not necessitate any cuts to the Pentagon's budget, which was music to the ears of Tom Cole, Elise Stefanik, and the many other defense hawks in our conference who raised objections to a reduction of all discretionary spending to 2022 levels.

Furthermore, we committed to use the upcoming debt limit fight as a point of leverage to push for these reductions or other commensurate fiscal reforms—an intentional framing that our lead policy staffer, Brittan Specht, proposed to give us added wiggle room to achieve these ends.

All of this would be done in addition to the items that had been floating in the ether for weeks but had not been formally agreed to yet, including the creation of a select committee to examine instances of weaponized government— negotiated by our general counsel, Machalagh Carr—and the reduction of the threshold for triggering a Motion to Vacate to any one member.

* * *

One by one, the Freedom Caucus brought members of the group of twenty holdouts into Majority Whip Emmer's conference room to review the parameters of the agreement. This was a painfully slow process, but it was seemingly the only way their group knew how to reach consensus.

At the same time, we rotated in pockets of rank-and-file members down the hall to preview the tentative agreement with them. This served two critical purposes. First, it let members of the group of two hundred know that Kevin still had a clear path forward, keeping morale high and helping our narrative of progress work its way into the bloodstream.

Second, it was always better for members to hear news from us than from the press. Presenting our rationale for the agreement in our own words and having as many members bought in on our thinking as possible would only serve to bolster the deal when details of it inevitably leaked.

Leaving the Capitol that evening, Kevin was asked by the press where things stood and how he felt about the action occurring behind the scenes.

"I felt very positive yesterday. I feel more positive today," he told them. "I think we had really good discussions."

Positive feelings were good. Discussions were better. But our window to turn those warm feelings and encouraging discussions into actual yes votes on the floor was closing rapidly.

The moment of truth was upon us, and we all knew it.

CHAPTER 17

JANUARY 6, 2023—MORNING SESSION: STOCKDALE PARADOX

The book *Good to Great* by Jim Collins was frequently quoted in the McCarthy operation.

While his lesson on "putting the right people in the right seat on the bus" was perhaps the most prominent—often cited as Kevin's inspiration for elevating Jim Jordan to be a ranking member back in 2018—there was another chapter that became our team's favorite in the weeks leading up to January 2023, what Collins referred to as the "Stockdale Paradox."

The concept, drawn from the experiences of Admiral Jim Stockdale during his eight years as a prisoner of war in Vietnam, captures the necessary mindset for enduring prolonged uncertainty, one that Stockdale himself described as follows:

"This is a very important lesson. You must never confuse faith that you will prevail in the end—which you can never afford to lose—with the discipline to confront the most brutal facts of your current reality, whatever they might be."

Patrick McHenry and I shared and reflected upon that passage with one another in the lead-up to the Speaker's fight, noting also Stockdale's unwavering belief that he would one day turn the ordeal into the defining moment of his life—one that he would not trade if given the choice. And on the chilly morning of January 6, 2023, I walked into the Capitol doing my best to heed Stockdale's lessons.

There's a good chance it won't happen today, I told myself. *That's all right. Just keep going.*

* * *

As promised the day before, Kevin started the morning by hosting a members-only conference call with all House Republicans to provide an update on where things stood and walk through details of the above-described agreement. Garret Graves, Patrick McHenry, and French Hill huddled together around the phone with us in the Speaker's office to offer extra color and help answer any questions.

"No one is being prioritized and no one is being punished," they repeated when pressed on the outlines of the agreement. "This is about moving forward together."

While that was underway, the Freedom Caucus hosted its own in-person meeting at Mark Meadows's Conservative Policy Institute up the street, which made me incredibly nervous. Though the HFC had left the building the night before in a good place, if there was anyone that could undo our progress in one fell swoop, it was probably Mark Meadows.

"We've got two hours," I told Chip Roy around 10 a.m. "I don't think we can go through another ballot without positive movement."

"I know," he responded. "I am trying to move the number."

Chip relayed that he thought twelve or thirteen of the Freedom Caucus holdouts were in play to vote for Kevin, but that they still needed more time. When I floated adjourning until 10 p.m. to buy them some extra time, Chip told me that Gaetz and the Never Kevin crew would vote with the Democrats to block us from taking a recess.

"Jesus. Okay, well then we're gonna need you to break for us at noon," I replied. "If you want to give the nominating speech, you can. And then we can have people talk during that vote."

He called me to say that he would vote for Kevin, but that since his name was later in the alphabet, he was not sure how much good it would do if it were only him. I told him that that was more than fine—we just absolutely needed his vote then and there.

* * *

As was the case every day before noon, I was scrambling to get myself together before going to the floor, including when it came to attire. I had worn my favorite tie on January 3 and my next-favorite ties the following two days. That Friday, I was looking for a simple red, white, and blue tie to match the navy blue suit I was wearing but could not seem to find it. Looking up at a clock that read 11:58 a.m., I reached for my next best option on the rack in my office: a bright orange tie that I would typically don on the rare Mondays that followed a Chicago Bears victory.

We're not gonna win today anyways, I told myself as I looped the admittedly loud-colored tie around my neck.

Sitting on the floor ahead of ballot twelve in what was now the longest Speaker's election since 1859, I still had no clue how things were going to pan out. As previously mentioned, our issue all week was that a number of our detractors came early in the alphabet. Today would be no different: By the end of the Bs, we would have a good idea of where things stood.

Once again, Andy Biggs of Arizona defected, voting for Jim Jordan. But then, something changed.

"Bishop of North Carolina?" the Clerk of the House queried.

Although Dan Bishop had been one of the final four representatives to negotiate on behalf of the Freedom Caucus, it was anyone's guess how he would vote that afternoon.

At the calling of his name, the gentleman from Charlotte slowly rose from his seat and cleared his throat—while I nervously held my breath.

"Kevin McCarthy," he stated.

My head immediately whipped over to the left to make sure my ears weren't deceiving me. It took a second to sink in for everyone else, as well, but upon realizing what had occurred, the Republican side of the aisle spontaneously burst into a standing ovation.

After all the talks, all the meetings, all the back-and-forth, the tide was now turning in our direction. Talk about a shot in the arm.

Kevin was not even on the floor yet and I texted him and the rest of our team to hurry out to see what was unfolding.

Next up was freshman Josh Brecheen of Oklahoma.

"Pending transformational rules changes . . . Kevin McCarthy," he stated.

Another ovation, this one louder than the last.

Cloud, Clyde, Donalds, Luna, and Miller of Illinois all voted McCarthy—each time followed by an ovation.

As much as anything, I relished the changing vibes on the Democratic side of the aisle. All week they had been giddy, enjoying the schadenfreude. Now, those grins were quickly being replaced by long faces that said, *Oh man, they're gonna figure this out.*

Clay Higgins of Louisiana, who for the past few days had been leading a prayer circle in the well of the House prior to us convening each day, held a Bible to his forehead after every flipped vote. Freshman Jerry Carl of Alabama began to scream out each one, holding up the count on his hands for the chamber to see.

"That's seven!" Carl yelled. "That's eight!"

Ralph Norman, the surprise Never Kevin from the autumn, flipped our way too. He was sitting only a few feet behind us, and I turned and pointed to him, mouthing "Thank you."

Andy Ogles of Tennessee and Scott Perry voted for Kevin, as did Chip Roy, true to his word. They were followed by Keith Self of Texas and Victoria Spartz of Indiana. Even Paul Gosar, who missed his name on the first pass, stated "Kevin McCarthy" from the back of the chamber, despite a last-minute desperation attempt by Matt Gaetz to lobby him the other way.

In total, fourteen members from the Freedom Caucus flipped to Kevin on ballot twelve, leaving us at 213, just five votes shy of the speakership.

Moreover, two additional yes votes would return to Washington later that day, with Ken Buck and Wesley Hunt due back in town around 9 p.m. For good measure, we arranged for a few members of Kevin's security detail to pick up Buck from Dulles International Airport and rush him back to the Capitol, while closely tracking Hunt's last-minute flight back from Texas.

* * *

In between ballots, our attention moved to Andy Harris, a senior appropriator from Maryland and a future chair of the Freedom Caucus himself. Harris voted for Jim Jordan on ballot twelve. But on paper, he was someone who fit in with the group of fourteen that had just flipped for us, and we were confidentially told that his vote was gettable.

Kevin and Harris retreated to a small office in the back corner of the floor, a space we staff referred to as the Room of Requirement from Harry Potter. It was a tiny room with only four small armchairs, but large enough to squeeze about a dozen people if needed—much more private than the Republican cloakroom where any number of members could butt into the conversation.

The group was joined by Kay Granger of Texas, chair of the Appropriations Committee, Rules Chair and future Appropriations Chair Tom Cole, along with Granger's staff director, Anne Marie Chotvacs, and our chief of staff, Dan Meyer.

Harris began by trying to leverage his vote for a guarantee that he would be named chair of the Appropriations subcommittee on Labor and Health and Human Services, one of the largest accounts in the federal budget and one of the most powerful panels on the spending committee.

Kevin calmly reminded him that no one had been promised a gavel and that Harris would be no exception. In response, Harris became emotional.

"I wanted this!" Harris cried.

"I know," Kevin responded. "You asked me for this before. I said no. It's still the same answer."

"If I can't do anything for my district, I am going to need to resign!" Harris bellowed, tears now running down his face. "Why am I even here?"

"Well, then you'll have to leave and we'll have a special election," Kevin replied. "I'm sorry you feel that way."

Slightly taken aback by the unfolding scene, Dan Meyer probed Harris further on this point.

"What is most important to your district?" Dan asked.

"Health care and agriculture," he responded.

Agriculture? Dan thought.

In fact, Harris had taken over as ranking member of the Agriculture subcommittee for the better part of the past year following the resignation of Nebraska Representative Jeff Fortenberry. And by all accounts, Harris's conduct and attitude had changed dramatically once he became a ranking member—or "cardinal," as the Appropriations subcommittee leads were known—assuming a greater leadership role on the committee and voting with the team when needed.

Dan conferred with Chairwoman Granger and her top aide in a brief aside about the current situation.

"Is Agriculture something you think is doable?" he asked them.

They checked their notes and told him that yes, they had actually already penciled Harris in for Agriculture but thought that this week's antics might have otherwise disqualified him for the spot. Dan told them that in the same way that no one was being prioritized, neither was anyone to be punished.

By that point, we were pushing thirty minutes of intermission and I went back to check on their status. When I walked into the room, Harris was wiping away tears from his eyes, which I was not sure whether to interpret as a good thing or a bad thing. But as he walked away, Kevin gave me a thumbs-up and told me to alert the front desk to run another ballot.

Sure enough, on ballot thirteen, Harris became our fifteenth flip of the afternoon. If you were to rewatch the video, you can see me standing behind him at the back of the chamber as his name was being called for good measure.

After he cast his vote, I saw Harris breathe a deep sigh of relief, as if a tremendous burden had been lifted off his shoulders. I could tell that he and the other Freedom Caucus guys were as worn down as we were. Now, they simply wanted it to be over.

* * *

With Kevin sitting at 214 votes, we were made aware that a new group was congregating in the Room of Requirement: the final six holdouts of Andy Biggs, Lauren Boebert, Eli Crane, Matt Gaetz, Bob Good, and Matt Rosendale.

While we had successfully broken the twenty, these six were among the most mercurial in our conference and would be by far the most difficult eggs to crack.

Some of the New York freshmen proposed—only half-jokingly—that they could barricade the six inside the room long enough for one more vote.

"That would work, right?" Anthony D'Esposito asked, himself a former NYPD detective. "Just give me a Phillips and they won't be out of there for a while!"

Fellow New Yorkers Nick LaLota and Marc Molinaro enthusiastically nodded in agreement.

I told them to hold their horses and relayed that I would check in with the Island of Misfit Toys myself.

Knocking on the door before entering, I encountered the six final hold-outs huddled together, looking dejected and aimless.

"Okay, guys, what do we think about an adjourn until later tonight?" I asked.

Biggs and Good questioned what the purpose of such a recess would be, to which I explained the Ken Buck and Wesley Hunt travel logistics, as well as what Roger Williams's wife was enduring. We—or should I say, they—were now keeping a lot of people from a lot of very personal things simply to prolong this losing fight.

Even so, they remained suspicious that the real reason we wanted to adjourn was to have the next round of votes at a time when more Democrats would be absent late in the night. After all, if any Democrats were absent, that would lower the threshold needed to win an outright majority.

"C'mon guys—you see them," I said. "They're as motivated as you are to not see Kevin become Speaker. They'll be here whenever we vote."

"Well what's going to change then?" they demanded.

"I would hope this group right here would sit down with Kevin and figure out a path forward," I said. "Maybe some of you answer 'present.' Or you can just say 'Hell no'—that works too."

In much the same way that Democratic absences would lower the 218 threshold, so too would any Republicans answering "present" or simply refusing to say a surname. In fact, Nancy Pelosi employed such a method to win the speakership with just 216 votes in 2021.

Kevin floated a similar strategy earlier in the week when pressed by the media as to how he could overcome his seemingly intractable math problem. In response, Matt Gaetz immediately begged off the idea, telling the press when asked whether he could be convinced to vote present: "[That's] so absurd that it's embarrassing you're asking me the question."

Rosendale shook his head violently at my suggestion, as well. "Nuh-uh, no way am I voting 'present'!" he said.

"That's not going to happen, John," Andy Biggs added through bloodshot eyes.

"Listen, I don't have the answer. You guys do," I replied. "But sooner or later, this is going to end."

With that, Gaetz asked if I could give the group a minute to have the room so they could deliberate together. After I waited for what felt like an eternity, Biggs found me on the floor and asked me to reenter the room. There, the group relayed that they would agree to adjourn until 10 p.m. and further added that Matt Gaetz and Lauren Boebert wanted to speak with Kevin.

Is this . . . is this actually happening? I wondered.

Hastily, I rushed to find Kevin on the floor and bring him back before they could change their minds.

"This is a good thing," I told him. "Stay calm. Whatever they say to you, take a breath first and let's see if we can work this out here and now."

* * *

As Kevin and I entered the Room of Requirement, Gaetz stood up to greet us.

"Congratulations, Mr. Speaker!" he said, extending his right hand to Kevin.

What the hell? I thought to myself.

"We made you earn it, but you are going to be our Speaker tonight," he continued.

As the four of us took a seat, Gaetz began the discussion. Specifically, he relayed that Lauren Boebert wanted to be considered for a seat on the Judiciary Committee, in part because she could not bear the thought of serving on the Oversight Committee with her public frenemy, Marjorie Taylor Greene, who would later call Boebert "a little bitch" to her face on the House floor.

Of the final six holdouts, Lauren Boebert was one of the biggest head-scratchers. Despite representing a safe district in the Aspen area that favored Republicans by approximately 6 percentage points, Boebert had won her most recent reelection by fewer than six hundred votes—one of the closest margins in the country—due in large part to local fatigue with her near-constant stream of antics and public embarrassments.

Rather than take the hint and change course, however, Boebert showed shockingly few signs of self-awareness. Instead, she chose to lean even more into the crazy crusade against Kevin, enduring several humiliating TV appearances along the way with everyone from Fox's Sean Hannity to MSNBC's Stephanie Ruhle.

"The way to get your numbers up is to deliver for the district and to make you a legislator," Kevin told Boebert. "I can help you with that," citing a forestry management bill of hers that he said he would work to move through the committee process.

It was hard to see how the past week had done any good for improving Boebert's image back home, and Kevin was now offering a real chance for her to turn things around.

Finally, Gaetz asked again that no retaliation be sought against himself or any of the holdouts, echoing his request from earlier in the week.

"Have you seen *Ted Lasso*?" Kevin asked. "Do you know what the happiest animal is? A goldfish, because it has a thirty-second memory. We need to have a goldfish memory about all of this if we want to get anything done."

"Okay, well then tonight, Lauren will vote for you and that will put you over the top," Gaetz replied.

I quickly interjected here to clarify the math. With the votes as they stood, we would need at least one more of them to either vote for Kevin or vote "present" in order to secure an outright majority. Gaetz seemed slightly confused by this basic arithmetic, but reassured us that he would sort it out with his group.

"Worst case, if it needs to be me, I'll go 'present,'" he added. "That would work, right?"

"Yes, if Lauren votes for Kevin and at least one other holdout votes present, we have a majority," I said.

With that, we all shook hands, stood up, and left—the elusive last votes seemingly and finally in hand.

* * *

"So what did they say?" our chief Dan Meyer inquired when he found me on the floor immediately afterward.

Still processing what had just went down, I took a moment to gather my emotions before speaking.

"It's over," I said slowly. "We're going to be Speaker."

His eyes began to well up, as did mine, and we shook hands. I rushed to share the news with Natalie Joyce and Matt Sparks, as well, and the three of us quietly celebrated in our office while breathing a collective sigh of relief. After all that we had been through together, what we had daydreamed of for years was now within our grasps.

As the news slowly began to trickle through our office, I stepped away onto the Speaker's balcony for a moment of reflection. Looking out over the National Mall, I mentally replayed all the highs and lows of the last ten years that had brought us to this point, from my earliest days as a college intern to all the craziness of the last few months.

Though a frigid January wind was whipping through, it might as well have been seventy-five degrees on a beach with how good I felt.

Even so, seven hours was a long time to wait until the House reconvened at 10 p.m. And as someone who had seen firsthand the truism that "time kills all deals," seven hours was more than enough time for mischief to brew.

CHAPTER 18

JANUARY 6, 2023—EVENING SESSION: SECOND DEATH

Our policy team often described dealmaking in Congress as a series of stages. Specifically, any budding agreement went from:

1. Necessary, to
2. Hard, to
3. Dead a first time, to
4. Seemingly impossible but both sides are still talking, to
5. Dead a second time, to
6. Everyone is angry but there is no other way out than to pass the deal.

My concern was that our deal with the Freedom Caucus had not yet died that second death. And before long, cracks began to emerge.

Tony Gonzales of Texas, a close ally of Steve Scalise, tweeted out that he would be a no on the House Rules package that was slated to be considered immediately after we elected a Speaker. Ditto for Nancy Mace of South Carolina, who told the press that she was also on the fence on the negotiated set of rules and procedures where much of our agreement with the Freedom Caucus lived—despite excoriating Matt Gaetz as a "political D-lister" only days earlier for his opposition to Kevin.

Without sufficient votes to pass the rules package, all of our work over the last weeks and months would be for naught and we would find ourselves stuck on the tarmac again, unable to proceed to the business of the House.

On the other side of the equation, Chip Roy was telling Garret Graves that some of his members wanted to reopen talks and make a few final tweaks to the agreement. Chip insisted that their votes for Kevin during the afternoon's series of votes were merely a show of good faith but that there was still more work to be done.

Then, around 4 p.m., I got a text followed by a call from an unknown 850 area code in Florida. You can imagine my dismay when I answered and heard the creepy voice of Matt Gaetz on the other end.

* * *

Gaetz began by telling me that despite his exhortations, his group of six was not budging from their posture of opposing Kevin.

"That's fine," I responded. "You agreed to go present if needed, so we don't need them to budge."

He pushed back and said that waiting for Monday would be better so he could have more time to get the entire group to come around. I reiterated that we could not be sure where our attendance would be on Monday and that tonight had to be the night.

"Then I'm going to need a sweetener. Say the Military Personnel gavel on HASC?" he said, using the shorthand for a subcommittee on the House Armed Services Committee that he now was demanding he be put in charge of.

"Sir, we can't do gavels," I said, "you know that."

Ironically—and perhaps a harbinger of things to come—Gaetz would have very likely received the promotion he was now trying to wrangle had he not decided to wage war against Kevin. In fact, one of the top Republican staffers on the committee told me at a Christmas party that winter that they were willing to elevate Gaetz if doing so would be helpful to us. After all, keeping Gaetz mollified could come in handy for the committee with conservatives when it came time to pass the yearly National Defense Authorization Act.

But we were now a long way from December. Not only was leading a subcommittee out, but Armed Services Chair Mike Rogers of Alabama had grown so incensed by what Gaetz was doing that he no longer wanted him to even serve on his committee anymore.

I suggested to Gaetz that we revisit the issue after the weekend when people might perhaps be a little more rested and in a better frame of mind.

"That doesn't sound promising," Gaetz replied before we hung up the phone.

A few hours later, he followed up in a text message, saying: "I'm thinking we need heads to cool, time to pass, rules to be read. I'd like to take no vote. Adjourn til noon Monday."

Needless to say, none of us were eager to entertain such a delay, one that very well could prove fatal to our fragile coalition if the flurry of activity and waffling over the last few hours was any indication.

"This is now officially above my pay grade," I replied. "I think you should come by to see Kevin."

* * *

When I entered Kevin's office, he was sitting at his desk with a few members from our communications team reviewing the introductory remarks that he would deliver to the chamber after being elected.

"Sir, we've got a problem," I said, explaining the back-and-forth I had with Gaetz and the promotion request that he was now on his way to our office with.

"He's bluffing," Kevin replied. "We've just got to wait him out."

By the time Gaetz arrived, he had backed off his request to lead the subcommittee, a rare moment of self-awareness reflecting how swampy such a move would look if actually executed. Instead, he simply continued to complain that he did not want to go it alone with Boebert for fear of being singled out by the right and needed more time to get his other guys on board with the plan.

"I have been trying, Mr. Speaker," Gaetz repeatedly said. "We all know it's over. But I want them with me on the vote."

"They are so mad at the fourteen," Gaetz continued, referring to the first fourteen Freedom Caucus members who broke ranks to support Kevin. "That's what's really going on, and they won't do what's best for their interest, the conference's best interest, or my best interest. It's not rational."

Once again, the obstructionists apparently never bothered to consider what steps two and three might be for getting out of the jam that they themselves created.

After about forty-five minutes of Kevin and Gaetz going around and around—including a call in from Sean Hannity pressing Gaetz to get it done and seal the deal that night—I excused myself from the office. Despite Kevin's confidence, I couldn't help but feel that this was the second death we had feared—except this time, we had already told friends and supporters to come to the Capitol at 10 p.m. to witness what we assumed would be the winning ballot.

Feeling queasy, I went and lay down on a couch in the office, being sure to spot the nearest trash can in case it would become necessary.

As we approached almost an hour, Gaetz finally left and Kevin emerged from his office.

"Okay, who else can we get of the six?" Kevin asked, indicating that Gaetz was going back on the commitment he had made just hours prior.

* * *

If Gaetz and Boebert were now out, that left us Andy Biggs, Bob Good, Eli Crane, and Matt Rosendale to work with.

Kevin called Andy Biggs first and decided to merge in a surprise third guest to the call.

"Andy, I'm merging in the president," Kevin said.

Before Biggs could realize what hit him, Donald Trump proceeded to unleash a tirade of expletives on the Arizona congressman.

"What the fuck are you guys doing?" Trump screamed at Biggs.

"Mr. President, Mr. President, we're just not going to change," Biggs stammered.

"I'll never fucking support you if you don't support Kevin!" he shouted back.

"I . . . Mr. President . . ." he tried to interject.

"Where's Crane?" Trump asked, referring to fellow Arizonan Eli Crane, who had won his primary election in large part thanks to Trump's endorsement in the race.

"He was in third place until I saved him," Trump shouted. "I'll find a fucking challenger to him so fast his head will spin."

Listening in on speakerphone, it was truly something to behold.

Nevertheless, despite this all-out verbal assault from Trump, the group hung up the phone with no resolution and no firm additional commitments to vote for Kevin.

Matt Rosendale and Bob Good ducked our calls next, perhaps having been given a heads-up about what awaited them on the other line.

Looking up at the clock on the wall, I realized it was now less than thirty minutes until our 10 p.m. reconvening time.

* * *

My phone buzzed nonstop with congratulatory texts and well-wishes from family, friends, and colleagues—past and present, near and far.

Supporters began to file into the building, our office filled with the smell of catered Five Guys burgers and fries. My wife, Giulia, even brought her parents and some of our closest friends to watch—all dressed for the occasion and ready to take their seats in the public gallery that overlooked the House floor.

Everyone was jubilant, smiling, giving each other high fives and hugs.

Unfortunately, I could not share in their joy. Instead, I sat alone in an empty office, feeling totally broken and helpless.

Unlike them, I knew the truth: We did not have the votes to win.

Abraham Lincoln is said to have remarked, "I have been driven many times upon my knees by the overwhelming conviction that I had nowhere else to go."

In that moment, I understood some small measure of what Lincoln meant.

Next to the Speaker's suite, behind the giant American flag that hangs off the Capitol Rotunda, is a small, nondenominational chapel. It has room for only two seats and two kneelers with a stained glass window in the front of the room depicting a kneeling George Washington in prayer.

My younger brother, Jeremy, was a deacon at the time, less than a year away from being ordained a Catholic priest. Earlier in the week, he had encouraged me to pray "The Surrender Novena"—which repeats "Jesus, I surrender myself to you. Take care of everything."

In that moment, there was no better lifeline to be able to call.

"Brother, I need your help, man," I said, starting to cry. "We're going to go out there in a little bit and we don't have the votes. I don't know what to do."

The tears were really flowing now.

"Can you pray with me?" I asked.

I knelt at the kneeler on the right side of the room and he began to walk me through some prayers intermixed with breathing exercises.

"Jesus" *inhale*—"I trust in you," *exhale*. "Jesus" *inhale*—"I trust in you," *exhale*.

"Heavenly Father, we praise you and we love you," Deacon Jeremy continued. "I ask you to be with John in this moment. If he is experiencing any fear, any doubts, any worries, Holy Spirit, I ask that you flood them away right now. Give him the gift of your peace and your presence."

"I pray for Kevin, I pray for John, and I pray for everyone on their staff. I pray for the gifts of perseverance, fortitude, and trust. Help us to trust that you never abandon us and that you have a plan for us."

After a few minutes of prayer, we ended with the Our Father and said our goodbyes. Right then, I felt an incredible wave of calmness come over me.

"Thank you, brother. I love you," I said, wiping my eyes and heading back to the main office.

* * *

It was now less than ten minutes until showtime, and the Speaker's office was anything but peaceful. Garret Graves informed us that he was coming up to the suite with Chip Roy, Scott Perry, Byron Donalds, and Dan Bishop to review the final parameters of the agreement, prompting our team to hastily prepare for their arrival.

As that group dotted the I's and crossed the T's on their respective sheets of notes, I was made aware that Matt Gaetz was standing at one of the microphones on the floor and appeared to be up to no good.

"I want to adjourn," he said to me as I hurried over to him. "We need to wait until Monday."

Unsure if he knew that he could make a motion to adjourn, I did my best to keep things on the rails and distract him until the balloting began.

"Sir, we're not doing that," I said, putting my hand on his shoulder and looking him dead in the eyes. "It needs to be tonight."

Safe to say, he did not take this news well and returned to his seat with a scowl that he would wear for the next hour or so, stewing in anger.

* * *

Ahead of ballot fourteen, we asked Kevin's longtime friend Patrick McHenry to deliver what we had presumed would be the final nominating speech for the week.

"He's unflinchingly optimistic. The glass is always half-full," McHenry began in his prepared remarks to a rare nighttime assembly of the House. "That's been a hell of a trait, especially this week."

Unfortunately, the House was about to test that unceasing sense of optimism.

As we entered the B's, Biggs once again voted for Jordan. This was certainly not a great sign, but it was not yet fatal as long as Boebert and Gaetz held up their end of the agreement.

"Boebert?" the Clerk of the House asked.

"Present," she said.

Motherfucker.

I had done my best to keep a straight face all week, but that one put me over the edge. While a brief applause broke out among the members, I knew that with Boebert going back on her word, we would need at least one of the other six to affirmatively vote for Kevin in order to achieve a majority.

Crane voted for Andy Biggs next, further shrinking our options. Then, it came to Gaetz.

"Gaetz?" the Clerk of the House queried.

No response.

"Gaetz?" she asked a second time.

The Floridian sat stone-faced and silent near the center aisle, letting the roll call pass him by. We sent our emissaries over to talk with him, including McHenry, Emmer, and Guy Reschenthaler. In the meantime, Good voted for Jordan and Rosendale voted for Biggs. That meant it would all come down to Gaetz.

* * *

At the end of each ballot, the reading clerk would call the names of anyone who failed to answer on the first pass, as well as inquire if anyone wanted to change their vote.

"Gaetz?" she asked, now for the third time.

"Present," he said.

This triggered another premature round of applause by our members thinking we had won. Instead, the tally stood at 216 for McCarthy, 212 for Jeffries, with four voting for other candidates, and two answering present—an exact, deadlocked tie when adding the votes for Jeffries with the votes for other candidates.

"You need to go talk to Gaetz," I told Kevin.

What followed was arguably the most dramatic sequence of events the entire week. With the eyes of the entire chamber upon him, Kevin calmly walked around the leadership desk, through the well, and up the center aisle toward where Gaetz was seated.

"Matt, Roger Williams's wife is dying," Kevin said.

"I told your staff that we needed to wait until Monday," Gaetz replied, pointing in my direction. "They said no and so that's why this is happening!"

Kevin continued to gently remind Matt of their discussion from earlier in the day, while running through all the other family and health emergencies that his colleagues were missing because of this impasse.

"I don't think you understand," Gaetz said. "That does not concern me whatsoever. Personal appeals have no effect on me."

In retrospect, that was probably the only completely honest statement he ever made to us and showed what a truly disturbing individual we were dealing with.

"Matt, come on. You've made your point." Kevin replied. "People have to go home."

"We talked about this, sir" I added after my name was invoked in the conversation, which only caused Gaetz to further spiral out of control.

"I told you right over there that I wanted to vote on Monday!" he bellowed at me. "You said that Kevin would never go for that and it was now or never!"

Although I wanted to punch Gaetz in the face for trying to twist my words, I was not about to let him use me as an excuse to cause even more of a scene. Instead, I slowly backed away to allow the members to try to sort it out among themselves. That was right about when Mike Rogers of Alabama decided that he wanted a word with Gaetz too.

"Matt, I won't forget this!" he shouted. "You hear me?"

Seeing this scene unfold, Richard Hudson of North Carolina tried to hold Mike Rogers back, only for his hands to slip and grab the Alabaman across the face. While this made for one of the most epic photos in recent congressional history, it caused quite a commotion in the process.

"He needs to get out of here, now!" one member screamed, as a wave of gasps rang out across the floor in response to what appeared to be a near-physical altercation.

Nearby, Clay Higgins of Louisiana began to cry. A few rows behind him, Texas freshman Morgan Luttrell—twin brother of famed "Lone Survivor" Marcus Luttrell—stared so intently at Matt Gaetz while reciting the Rosary that some feared he might also try to take matters into his own hands.

In case it was not already clear, we had officially devolved into full-blown Lord of the Flies.

* * *

Unbeknownst to all of us, there was another conversation happening in a separate corner of the floor at that very moment that almost broke the logjam—one that has gone unreported until now involving Democrat Marcy Kaptur of Ohio, the longest-serving woman in the history of Congress.

Witnessing this chaos unfold, Kaptur had wandered over to our side of the aisle to begin talking with Mike Turner, her fellow Ohio delegation mate and chair of the Intelligence Committee.

"This isn't right, Mike," she told him, shaking her head.

"Marcy, if you want, you can end this right now," Turner replied. "I'll go to the well with you and we can change your vote and this will all be over."

While we remained focused on getting a majority through Republican votes, any small handful of Democrats could have also been enough to defect and put Kevin over the top—a fact our allies were sure to share with their friends across the aisle. And though this type of crossover vote was unprecedented in modern times, so too was a multi-ballot contest for Speaker that appeared to have no clear end in sight.

Indeed, Kaptur seemed to be seriously contemplating such a bipartisan gesture, so much so that members of the Democratic floor team caught wind of her wavering stance and were told to keep an eye on her. Before she and Turner could make any sort of move to the well to change her vote, Democratic Whip Katherine Clark of Massachusetts swooped in like "a witch on a broom" as one member later recalled, intercepting Marcy and angrily talking her out of the plan.

After a long and animated conversation between the two, Marcy agreed to back down and dejectedly walked back to the Democratic left side of the chamber. There would be no bipartisan vote that day. The stalemate would continue.

* * *

As ballot fourteen officially drew to a close, the Clerk of the House took to the podium.

"The tellers agree in their tallies that the total number of votes cast is 432—of which the honorable Kevin McCarthy of the State of California has received 216," she declared to the now shell-shocked chamber.

This script was followed by what was quickly becoming one of my least favorite sentences in the English language: "No Member-elect having received a majority of the votes cast, a Speaker has not been elected."

In a moment of anger, I found Chip Roy and Scott Perry on the floor and fumed to them about this latest setback.

"We had an understanding and they broke it," I told them, detailing what Boebert and Gaetz had said they were going to do only hours earlier. "I don't know how we can expect to operate like this."

As we huddled with Kevin to contemplate our next move, Patrick McHenry came over to offer his opinion.

Widely recognized as one of the best whips in the House, Patrick had been talking extensively with Gaetz both during the ballot and in the aftermath. His gut instincts rivaled only Kevin's for reading other members—and we trusted he would give us sound advice.

"It was a hell of a time just to get him to go present, Kevin," he told us.

Patrick added that Gaetz was liable to only dig in further if we continued to ballot into the night, but that his present vote should be viewed a sign of progress that made victory all-but-inevitable.

"Let them fundraise for a few more days, then get them to cave on Monday," Patrick reasoned.

While I rarely disagreed with Patrick, my heart sunk at this assessment. Not only did that mean two more sleepless nights and famished days for our team, but a weekend was a long time for something to go wrong.

"It's okay, I didn't want to win on January 6th anyways," Kevin joked.

Though our team remained divided on the decision and a few of us did our best to stall, Kevin eventually gave his okay to McHenry to take to the microphone.

"Madam Clerk, I move that we adjourn until noon Monday," McHenry said.

The chamber responded with a loud mix of yeas and nays and we reluctantly encouraged our members to vote yes. Almost immediately, however, a large group of members came over to express their reservations about this course of action.

"I think this is a bad idea, John," one of my good friends, Darin LaHood of Illinois, told me.

Dusty Johnson of South Dakota and Dave Joyce of Ohio also registered their displeasure, as did the rowdy New York aisle.

"We have them on the ropes," the Long Islanders shouted. "Let's vote all night!"

"It's all good," Kevin reassured them. "We'll just win on Monday."

I looked up and saw my wife and in-laws leaving their seats in the gallery to go home. It was nearly midnight at that point and all I could think about was that we had failed yet again.

* * *

As the vote on adjourning neared a close, however, I happened to notice Matt Gaetz reemerge onto the floor from the back of the chamber. He made a beeline over to Kevin, who was standing in the well of the House cheerily conversing with other members and trying to keep morale high.

"We're good," Gaetz told him. "We'll do it tonight."

To this day, we still do not know what changed their minds. Gaetz claimed that the adjourn vote awakened them to the fact that they, too, would need to endure the stress of this race for two more days. Meanwhile, Bob Good claimed that it was him who finally broke and encouraged the entire group to vote present.

"When there were four of us left, we knew that we could not win," Eli Crane of Arizona later recalled.

Whatever the case, I heard all I needed to hear and quickly turned my attention to defeating the very motion to adjourn that we had supported only minutes earlier. The timer on the vote had already reached zero and the motion was prevailing, which would have put us into recess until Monday the second the Clerk of the House banged the gavel down.

"Vote no! Vote no!" I screamed, running up the aisle and pointing my thumbs downward.

Fortunately, our members did not need much urging, and a stampede of Republicans flooded the well to grab red voting cards to signal their change of vote.

A loud cheer arose from the public gallery above as our patrons watched the unfolding scene, realizing something must have changed.

Indeed, we had a pulse.

JANUARY 7, 2023—MR. SPEAKER

"The eyes of the world, the eyes of America, are on this body right now," Bruce Westerman of Arkansas began, the final nominating speech of the week and the shortest by far.

"What America needs, what this body needs, is a lot less talk and a lot more action," he continued, paraphrasing Toby Keith. "So at the direction of the Republican conference, I advance the name of Kevin McCarthy as the next Speaker of the House for the 118th Congress!"

A boisterous applause broke out, along with chants of "one more time" on our side of the chamber.

I made sure to sneak into the Speaker's lobby to frantically call my wife.

"Come back," I told her. "We're going to win for real this time!"

At the beginning of the week, our cloakroom staff had created and printed dozens of mock tally sheets with every member's name on them so we could manually keep track during each roll call. We handed them out to interested members and floor staffers to make sure our counts were accurate after each ballot.

Knowing it could be a while, I had taken a large handful that Tuesday for myself and stored them in the drawer where Kevin and I sat each day. But when the fifteenth ballot began and I went to grab a new tally sheet, I realized it was the last one I had in the drawer—the fifteenth.

Days later, it also dawned upon me that a book of prayers to St. Rita— Saint of Impossible Dreams—that I devoted myself to when applying to Stanford and that my brother encouraged me to reread included a series of prayers to be recited over a course of successive days. The number of prayers? You guessed it: fifteen.

"The answer was sitting in front of us the whole time," I later told Kevin.

* * *

At 12:37 a.m., on January 7, 2023, Kevin Owen McCarthy was elected the 55th Speaker of the House.

For the first time all week, we allowed ourselves to sit back, smile, and enjoy a round of balloting. All six of the final holdouts voted present, meaning that Kevin's 216 votes were finally enough to secure a majority of those voting by surname.

"That's what Pelosi got," he exclaimed to me when the final tally was read, ever competitive with his Golden State counterpart.

A group of members immediately mobbed him at the leadership desk, from longtime friends to newly elected freshmen. Some asked him to sign their tally sheets and hats, and one even jokingly asked him to sign the back of her dress.

When all the members had finished their congratulations, I slapped him on the back.

"My man!" he exclaimed.

I responded with the two words that I had been waiting to say for over a decade: "Mr. Speaker."

The loud cheer emanating from the public gallery stocked with our supporters rose to a crescendo as we hugged and I pointed both index fingers at him. It was a moment I will never forget.

* * *

As the escort committee was assembling, I was finally free to roam the floor. Members offered their congratulations to our team, along with more hugs left and right. The most meaningful embraces, though, were with my wife, Giulia, who made her way down to the floor using her staff ID badge, and the members of our floor team and senior staff. We had been on this ride together for over a decade now and made it out on the other side alive.

Traditionally, the escort committee would be comprised of all the members of the state delegation of the Speaker-elect—in this instance, California—along with the bipartisan members of House leadership. In a break from tradition, however, Kevin requested a few last-minute additions in the form of the eight members of the final negotiating team: Patrick McHenry, Garret Graves, Tom Emmer, and French Hill, along with Chip Roy, Scott Perry, Byron Donalds, and Dan Bishop. I sensed the Freedom Caucus guys were particularly touched by the gesture.

Around 1:30 a.m., after enduring a winding introductory speech from Democratic Leader Hakeem Jeffries, Kevin was finally handed the Speaker's gavel.

"Well, that was easy, huh?" he began upon taking the podium. "I never thought we'd get up here."

That line was ad-libbed, but as you now know, was more true than many people might have realized.

There were many days and hours when our situation looked bleak, particularly over that final week. At countless junctures, it would have been so much easier to ring the bell and throw in the towel. To simply walk away and end the pain. But I am proud to have worked for someone who exemplified patience, perseverance, and fortitude under pressure—and did it all with a smile on his face.

"I may not know all of you. Some of you are new," Kevin told the chamber as he concluded his remarks. "But I hope one thing is clear after this week: I never give up."

The members stood and roared in approval.

* * *

By the time we got back to our office, the Architect of the Capitol had already installed a freshly painted wood sign above our suite on the second floor: "Speaker of the House Kevin McCarthy."

A tunnel of staffers and supporters lined the hallway, and a huge cheer erupted every time someone walked into the office. Thankfully, our front-office team had a few crates of champagne wheeled in at the last minute, and we toasted in the conference room around 2 a.m.

The paintings of Washington Crossing the Delaware, Reagan, and Lincoln looked on while Queen's "We Are the Champions" and "I Won't Back Down" by Tom Petty and the Heartbreakers blasted on the loudspeakers, members and staff filling the room shoulder to shoulder.

After a brief speech from Kevin, James Min, one of the most beloved staffers on Team McCarthy, was given the opportunity to offer a toast.

"Actions speak louder than words," he said, proceeding to perform his famous "chuggies" routine, downing a champagne flute with ease.

Even Kevin, who I had only seen sip alcohol once or twice before, indulged a little bit, drinking a glass of bubbles alongside his wife and family before leaving the Capitol for a well-earned night of rest.

Our team, meanwhile, partied until the wee hours of the morning, with cigars on the Speaker's balcony, champagne in the conference room, and music and dancing throughout the hallways and various offices of the Speaker's suite.

I know those office walls had seen their fair share of history over the years, but I have to imagine our party was one of the best.

For us staffers, this was our version of the locker room celebration after winning the World Series. The only thing I could compare that feeling of unbridled bliss to would have been my wedding. Tons of congratulatory texts and calls were flooding in, but I couldn't care less to check my phone. Instead, all of the people who had worked so hard for years and even decades to make it happen were together in one place, celebrating.

We did it.

* * *

At around 6 a.m., I found myself in my favorite place in the Capitol: all alone under the dome of the rotunda.

During a typical day, that room was abuzz with tourists and visitors from every state and around the world, marveling at the massive paintings and carved reliefs on the walls, the life-size statues of our nation's most famous leaders that encircled the floor, and the ornate fresco depicting George Washington being raised into heaven that overlooked it all.

After hours, however, when everyone had left the building, the room fell completely still and I often found myself sitting alone on one of its benches, admiring the views while quietly reflecting on the happenings of the day.

Sometimes, it almost felt as if the statues were prepared to pull a *Night at the Museum* and come alive to begin conversing with one another—perhaps Martin Luther King Jr. talking about civil rights with Abraham Lincoln, Andrew Jackson and Dwight D. Eisenhower swapping war stories, or Ronald Reagan comparing notes with Thomas Jefferson about the ideals upon which our nation was founded.

The week before our wedding, in fact, Giulia and I gave Capitol tours to a number of our family and friends who made their way to Washington for the festivities. I was later told that upon entering the rotunda, my grandpa—himself an immigrant who came to America from Bolivia alone at age fifteen—asked a colleague of mine how it was determined which statues made it into this place of honor. My colleague, Cullen Murphy, explained that each state sent two statues to the Capitol, the most prominent of which made their way into the rotunda.

My grandpa replied: "They're going to have a statue of John in here one day. Watch."

Well, Grandpa, I am not so sure if that will be the case. But as I walked out of the Capitol early that morning, I felt that we had indeed achieved something that would be remembered. And no one could ever take that away from us.

PART IV
A HOUSE DIVIDED

CHAPTER 20

FULL FAITH AND CREDIT

The days and weeks that followed were quite the whirlwind.

I briefly became a meme on Twitter known as "Orange Tie Guy," while the confrontation between Matt Gaetz and Mike Rogers was repurposed into a comedic "Bad Lip Reading" video that garnered over four million views on YouTube.

The sheer number of people who were captivated by the unfolding events of that week was astonishing. For a time, complete strangers waved to me and introduced themselves on the streets of Washington. One man asked me to sign a baseball for him. Not exactly the autographs I envisioned giving out when I was a kid with dreams of playing shortstop for the Chicago White Sox, but still pretty cool.

Even Pope Francis confided in Kevin during a private audience that he and his staff watched ballot after ballot on television from his papal offices inside the Vatican. After all, multi-ballot elections are the rule, not the exception, when choosing a Pope—minus the C-SPAN cameras, of course.

There was little time to bask in the glow, however. Only two weeks after our victory, the United States hit its legal "debt ceiling"—the maximum amount of borrowing allowable by law—which triggered the Treasury Department to begin taking "extraordinary measures" to prevent a first-ever credit default.

"I respectfully urge Congress to act promptly to protect the full faith and credit of the United States," Treasury Secretary Janet Yellen wrote to the Speaker on January 19.

Her letter also indicated that the Treasury Department would only be able to sustain such extraordinary measures into the summer, meaning that a default "X date" could come as early as June.

As if summoned by fate, the same intimidating beast that loomed over our 2015 bid for Speaker—a showdown to raise the debt ceiling under a Democratic president—now once again reared its ugly head. But whereas that first encounter found us timid and uncertain, we would not back down again. This time, we were ready for the fight.

* * *

As anyone who has dealt with this issue in the past can attest, the debt limit is mentally all-consuming, particularly during periods of divided government. That meant for the first half of 2023, nearly all of my waking thoughts—morning, noon, and night—somehow drifted back to the debt ceiling.

Back in 2011, Speaker Boehner and House Republicans had their own staring contest with President Obama over the debt limit. That episode of brinksmanship devolved into a full-blown crisis, one that was resolved with only days to spare. US stock markets saw their most volatile week since the Great Recession, with steep declines across the board. Shortly thereafter, credit-rating agency S&P downgraded the creditworthiness of the United States for the first time in our nation's history.

In the aftermath, President Obama vowed to never again negotiate around the debt ceiling, a position that was adopted by his then–Vice President Joe Biden when he ascended to the White House himself in 2021.

Having served as majority whip during the 2011 crisis, Kevin was no stranger to the issue. In private, he was committed to ensuring that America did not default. But he was also committed to not settling for a so-called "clean" debt ceiling increase that lacked meaningful spending cuts or fiscal reforms.

"The two greatest threats to America are our debt and China," Kevin often repeated.

In that regard, simply writing another blank check would be an equally irresponsible move in his eyes as America's massive national debt continued to balloon.

Between President Biden's position of not negotiating over the debt ceiling and our posture of only raising the debt ceiling in tandem with reforms, something would have to give—and the early prognostications did not favor us.

"We're going to win this fight, and it's going to be a clean debt ceiling," Senate Majority Leader Chuck Schumer smugly predicted during a Sunday show interview with ABC's George Stephanopoulos in early February, echoing what was the conventionally held wisdom in Washington at that time, including among certain Republican circles.

"I don't think they'll be able to pass a debt limit increase, which leaves them without a whole lot of leverage to make demands of the administration," added Brendan Buck, a former adviser to Speakers Boehner and Ryan. "So I think Kevin McCarthy will probably end up needing to go to the White House without a whole lot in his back pocket."

Even so, we remained committed to our objective. To prepare, Kevin consulted with a wide variety of experts and veterans in the arena for their thoughts and advice. Many were helpful, but few as much so as former Speaker Newt Gingrich, who visited Kevin during his second week on the job for what turned into an hour-long strategy session almost entirely about the debt limit.

Gingrich reasoned correctly that Biden's stance was a losing one with the public.

"Americans expect their leaders to sit down, negotiate, and find common ground," he said, citing a January Rasmussen poll that found only 24 percent of Americans believed the debt ceiling should be raised without spending cuts, which was the stated position of the White House.

"Forcing Biden to negotiate changes everything," Kevin agreed.

"All you need to do is get him to negotiate," Gingrich stated, noting that Kevin as Speaker should only negotiate directly with the president and no one else. "Once he agrees to negotiate, you will have already won."

"What are the odds he will negotiate?" I asked them both, more than a little concerned about undertaking yet another high-stakes game of chicken.

"One hundred percent," Gingrich confidently replied.

* * *

After Kevin requested and received a meeting with the president on February 1—a meeting that our side left feeling fairly optimistic—the White House proceeded to go completely dark on us, hewing instead to Senate Majority Leader Schumer's continued position of non-negotiation.

That proved to be a tactical error on their part, as Speaker McCarthy cheerfully and persistently maintained over the next hundred or so days that the only way forward was for him and the president to sit down and responsibly work this out.

Members of the media who had not paid close attention during Kevin's years leading the House minority were especially stunned by his calm demeanor and ability to stay on message during his freewheeling and frequent gaggles with the Capitol Hill press corps. In the hallways, on TV, and even on the floor of the New York Stock Exchange, Kevin was ubiquitous—much to the chagrin of the Biden administration, which gradually realized it was being outmaneuvered and losing the public relations battle.

Inside the Republican conference, our members increasingly had our back, as well.

"We're really gratified to see the Speaker send a strong message to the President of the United States that it will be the president who chooses to gamble with the possibility of default, not the United States House of Representatives," Chip Roy told the press.

* * *

In early March, counselor to the president Steve Ricchetti, along with Biden's head of legislative affairs, Louisa Terrell, summoned a few of us to the West Wing for a strictly confidential meeting to discuss "upcoming legislative deadlines."

Our chief of staff, Dan Meyer, Kevin's top policy aide, Brittan Specht, and myself crammed into the back of a DC taxi on an unseasonably hot Washington spring day for what would be the first of many shuttles back and forth between Biden's team and ours over the coming weeks and months in pursuit of an elusive agreement to resolve the debt ceiling.

While the details remained in flux—Ricchetti, for example, continued to insist that the debt ceiling would need to be clean but that other negotiated items could perhaps be passed in tandem—the White House made clear that we would need to more plainly articulate what it was we were seeking in a negotiation before they could go any further.

Fresh off our own struggle with the Freedom Caucus and their frustratingly vague demands for "transformational change," I could empathize with where the White House was coming from. They were open to negotiating—but it was up to us to present an opening bid.

"It doesn't need to be a budget," Ricchetti told us. "But it needs to be something on paper that we can actually present to the president and negotiate around."

Shortly thereafter, Kevin sent a March 28 letter to the president outlining our areas of focus, which included reducing nondefense government spending to pre-inflationary levels, limiting out-year growth of federal spending, rescinding unspent COVID-19 funds, increasing work requirements on those without dependents who received certain forms of government assistance, taking measures to lower energy costs, and increasing security at the US-Mexico border.

Those particular line items were not chosen at random. Instead, they had emerged through a string of member listening sessions hosted by Majority Whip Tom Emmer and Chief Deputy Whip Guy Reschenthaler, along with a series of Five Families meetings held by newly appointed Chairman of the Elected Leadership Committee, Garret Graves—a position that Kevin revived for his new aide-de-camp from Louisiana.

As the specifics began to take shape, Democrats shifted their line of attack from "we will not negotiate" to "show us your plan," hoping we would overreach and cut politically sensitive areas of the budget like Social Security, Medicare, or veterans' spending, thereby enabling them to regain the upper hand in the court of public opinion.

Our members remained eager to assist in the formation and promotion of our proposal, as well. During that year's member retreat in Orlando, Florida, I texted back and forth with ally Dusty Johnson of South Dakota, who encouraged us to more clearly distill our position into a shorthand that could be repeated by all members.

"The way we address our debt is threefold: Limit Spending, Save Taxpayer Dollars, and Grow the Economy," I told him. "Any proposal that fits in one of those categories that can pass muster in our conference should be in the mix."

"Yes. This is perfect," he replied. "This is the way."

Admittedly, this phraseology was not entirely novel. The last time House Republicans managed to put together enough votes on their own for a bill to raise the debt ceiling was in 2011 under a different three-point plan dubbed Cut, Cap, and Balance. Twelve years later, the McCarthy debt ceiling plan would become known as Limit, Save, Grow.

* * *

The week after Easter, Kevin called and said that he wanted to pass a debt ceiling bill through the House by the end of April. The White House had still yet to formally begin negotiations and Kevin was through with the passive back-and-forth letters and shuttle diplomacy via staff. Only passing a bill would give us true leverage and force the White House and Senate to take us seriously, he reasoned.

"Do you think we can pass it?" he asked.

"Honestly, I think we can get there," I replied.

"Emmer thinks so too."

"All right then, we'll get the gears moving."

The day of the vote, however, we found ourselves in familiar territory, still scrambling to find 218 yeses.

Our old friend Matt Gaetz—despite being a loud advocate in our Five Families meetings for making the debt ceiling a single-issue fight about work requirements—raised a last-minute objection to the wording of the bill text.

"An essential element to get my vote for any increase in the debt limit would be enacting work requirements starting in fiscal year 2024—NOT 2025 as the legislation is currently written. Otherwise, it's a no vote from me," he tweeted the night before the vote was slated to occur.

He went on CNN that same evening to claim there were at least eight holdouts on the bill.

"I do not expect there will be a vote tomorrow as planned on the McCarthy debt limit increase," he stated.

Unbeknownst to him, we were working behind the scenes to harmonize the very implementation dates he objected to, which a rational human being might assume would assuage his concerns. But as you now know, nothing with Gaetz was ever easy.

"I will not vote for this bill today," he repeatedly told Kevin in a closed-door meeting in the Speaker's office a few hours before the scheduled vote. "It cannot be today."

As per usual, taking yes for an answer was never his strong suit. And even though we had been counting on securing Gaetz's vote, Kevin felt that waiting could prove fatal and that we might never have a better chance to pass the bill than we did that day.

"Fuck him," Kevin told us after Gaetz left. "Let's go."

Following a last-minute meeting with our leadership team to crunch the whip check, Kevin decided to roll the dice, a gamble that paid off as the Limit, Save, Grow Act of 2023 passed the House with not a single vote to spare. If you watch the tape, you'll see me dragging fabulist Congressman George Santos of New York to the Speaker's dais to submit the winning vote.

It was April 26, my thirty-second birthday.

* * *

This surprise success completely defied the DC press corps and the prevailing groupthink in Washington. Moreover, it provided a much-needed burst of momentum for us and left the White House with no other avenue than to go through House Republicans to reach a negotiated settlement.

Just over a month later, after weeks of meetings at the staff level and intense negotiations between our team and the White House, the Fiscal Responsibility Act was passed and signed into law—raising the debt ceiling for the remainder of the Congress in exchange for policy concessions and spending caps that represented the single largest deficit-reduction bill in history.

Kevin tapped close allies Garret Graves and Patrick McHenry to be our lead negotiators across the table from the White House's Steve Ricchetti, Louisa Terrell, and Office of Management and Budget Director Shalanda

Young, herself a former House staffer I had gotten to know during her time as the Democratic staff director for the Committee on Appropriations.

As is required, the talks died at least once or twice along the way. But one late night, after members of both of our teams had indulged in a few adult beverages in the Speaker's conference room, Shalanda and I were able to land on a 1 percent reduction in federal spending should all twelve appropriations bills not be enacted on time.

She originally proposed a flat freeze, our side tried for a 2 percent reduction, and we eventually settled on the 1 percent cut—the same 1 percent that I remembered Thomas Massie of Kentucky floating during our organizing meetings in the fall. This trigger proved to be one of the linchpins of the agreement, with Massie, himself, delivering the decisive vote to approve the measure through the House Rules committee a few weeks later, while Chip Roy and Ralph Norman voted with the Democrats to attempt to block the measure just days before a first-ever default.

In the end, the bill passed the House with suspension-worthy numbers, 314–117, and saw Republicans support the measure by a greater than two-to-one ratio, 149–71. It included such Republican priorities as reforms to streamline the federal permitting process, language that Garret Graves secured at the buzzer after countless hours of back-and-forth with the White House. Likewise, it restarted payments on Biden's student loan pause and updated state rolls for work requirements, thanks to the tenacity of Patrick McHenry. The three titles of the bill were Limit, Save, and Grow, just as we drew it up.

By any objective standard, the bill was a win, particularly in the face of a Democratic Senate and White House.

But as you might have gathered, we were not living in objective times.

CHAPTER 21

"TO WHOM IT MAY CONCERN"

Toward the end of the August recess, I was enjoying a family trip abroad with my wife and in-laws when Kevin forwarded a troubling tweet from Matt Gaetz that ended by saying "we are going to have to seize the initiative and make some changes."

I hastily sent a response from my hotel room outlining ways in which we could get back on the offense for our conference's priorities, including by tying any future requests from the Biden administration for Ukraine aid to stricter border security policies that were broadly desired among our members.

The problem, of course, was that Gaetz was not interested in policy. Instead, he sensed discontent in the ranks in the aftermath of the debt ceiling and saw a new opportunity to achieve what he had failed to do in January: block Kevin McCarthy from serving as Speaker.

Moreover—and unbeknownst to us at the time—Gaetz was also seemingly being driven by an agenda completely unrelated to the business of Congress: specifically, halting an ongoing bipartisan House Ethics Committee investigation into his alleged sexual conduct with a minor. The panel had resumed its work in May 2023 following the Justice Department's decision to not bring formal charges against the Florida representative, and Gaetz apparently believed that Kevin was responsible for the continuation of his case.

If there were any doubts as to his intentions, those were resolved when an outside ally tweeted at Gaetz that he should blame himself rather than Kevin for the independent investigation that began long before we took office.

Gaetz sent a screenshot of the tweet to Kevin, calling it a "very poor decision" for the ally to invoke the Ethics Committee inquiry. He ended his text with an ominous message: "See you soon."

* * *

Until then, I had held out some hope that at least a few reasonable Democrats might have emerged to protect the institution if and when a vacate vote was triggered. After all, under Kevin's leadership, the House had avoided default, kept the government open, and worked in a bipartisan fashion on such issues as countering China and addressing artificial intelligence.

Even amid the inevitable instances of partisan politics, Kevin had established a far more straightforward and workmanlike relationship with Minority Leader Hakeem Jeffries of New York—usually conducted over text between the two fifty-something-year-old lawmakers—than he ever had with Nancy Pelosi.

For example, when Kevin told Jeffries that he would not be reappointing Californians Adam Schiff and Eric Swalwell to serve on the House Intelligence Committee, Jeffries said that he understood and simply asked that we allow him to first send a public letter to demonstrate that he was "fighting" for his members. After that, he would let us deny their committee assignments without any further floor antics or demonstrations.

Maybe this is a guy we can work with, I cautiously thought to myself.

As the potential for a vacate vote became more real, Jeffries admitted to Kevin in private that he was not eager to vote with Matt Gaetz on such an important measure. Even so, I sensed that he and his senior staff were too inexperienced in House leadership to know what, if anything, they were supposed to ask for in exchange for releasing Democratic votes on a question of that magnitude.

"You have five families, Kevin. I've got eleven," Jeffries noted, a nod to the various interest and identity groups that make up the House Democratic

Caucus—all of whom Jeffries would need to consult with and court so as to not tarnish his own chances of one day becoming Speaker.

Internally, Kevin was equally clear-eyed about the challenges of a crossover vote.

"There's two types of leaders: a thermometer and a thermostat," he would tell us, drawing a distinction between those who can change the temperature and those who merely sit back to see which way the wind is blowing. "Hakeem is a thermometer."

In fairness to the Jeffries team, I cannot imagine we would have been likely to step in to save him or Nancy Pelosi if the shoe were on the other foot. After all, if you're trying to take back the House, it's hard to pass on a chance to take out the other party's top fundraiser and recruiter.

Moreover, Kevin made clear that he felt the vote was strictly about the institution, and that he was not prepared to offer any concessions to Democrats in exchange for their support on a motion to table Gaetz's resolution. Doing so would have effectively amounted to trading one gun to our head for another, to say nothing of the headlines and erosion within our own party that was likely to have followed were we to cut any sort of power-sharing agreement with the Democrats.

The morning of the vacate vote, Kevin absolved Jeffries of any lingering culpability the minority leader might have felt for the decision.

"Just my opinion—don't split your conference," Kevin texted the New York Democrat. "This is my fight in my party."

* * *

On October 2, Matt Gaetz formally introduced his Motion to Vacate resolution against Kevin. That same day, he also directed his lawyers to transmit a long-overdue response to House Ethics Committee investigators—a convergence of events that, in retrospect, seems far from coincidental.

Unlike the resolution Mark Meadows drafted against Speaker Boehner in 2015 detailing over two pages of perceived slights and violations, Gaetz did not even bother to include a single line of explanation for why Kevin deserved to be recalled.

Ostensibly, our sin was passing a routine thirty-day clean extension of government funding.* Despite knowing full well that doing so could trigger a vote that would end his political career, Kevin made the call he felt was right, keeping the government open and our troops paid rather than stumbling into a pointless shutdown.

"If I'm gonna go down, it's gonna be leading," he remarked to our team.

We even managed to roll the Senate in the process for good measure, a rare feat for any House Speaker. On a different day, in a different political climate, it would have been a story of victory.

Instead, the following day, Kevin once again was forced to fall on his sword.

We opted to conduct the vacate vote via a manual roll call—the same process used for the fifteen ballots back in January, with members standing one-by-one alphabetically—rather than the more customary electronic voting system.

If nothing else, we wanted the entire House to internalize the gravity of what they were undertaking and perhaps feel a little guilty for doing so. I was later told that when Steny Hoyer's name was called, Kevin's longtime friend from Maryland needed another Democratic member to hold his hand as he slowly stood to regretfully cast his "aye" vote from the far back corner of the chamber.

In the end, the vote to remove Kevin was 216–210, with only eight Republicans joining all House Democrats to recall a sitting Speaker for the first time in history, plunging the chamber headlong into a chaotic, leaderless three-week search for a replacement.

* * *

First to throw his hat in the ring was Majority Leader Steve Scalise of Louisiana. A few members of our team overheard Scalise staffers celebrating the night Kevin was removed, with drinks flowing in the majority leader's suite of offices

---

*   In total, the House and Senate would pass seven additional continuing resolutions at essentially the same funding level from 2023 to 2025.

as Steve started to work the phones for his own bid for Speaker mere hours after the vacate vote.

The champagne was better kept on ice, however, as Scalise was forced to abandon his run due to a lack of support less than ten days later, adding another name to the Curse of the Majority Leader.

Next up was Jim Jordan of Ohio, the Chair of the Judiciary Committee and a founding member of the House Freedom Caucus. Jim had come in second to Scalise during the first round of internal voting and seemed poised to capture the gavel—that is, until allies of Scalise worked to undermine his bid as retribution for their preferred candidate losing.

After three rounds of voting on the House floor in which he failed to garner the necessary majority, Jim Jordan announced that he, too, would be withdrawing his name from consideration for the job.

Majority Whip Tom Emmer, the number three in leadership, then put himself forward. Certain elements of the Freedom Caucus had floated Emmer's name internally as their choice for the job from the get-go, which made it seem like the well-respected Minnesotan would be on a glide path as the House concluded its second week without a Speaker.

Even so, over two dozen Freedom Caucus Members turned around and publicly pledged that they were not yet ready to support the whip's bid, which was quickly followed by a post from former President Trump that put the nail in the coffin. A few hours after receiving the nomination, Emmer became the latest casualty of the increasingly disorganized and ever-restless House Republican conference.

* * *

For a brief period of time, it seemed like the House might turn to an unconventional method of resolving the stalemate—namely, voting to empower "Speaker Pro Tempore" Patrick McHenry of North Carolina.

The night before the vacate vote, I informed McHenry that he was the first individual named on a secret list submitted by Kevin for lawmakers to serve as Speaker on an acting basis were a vacancy ever to arise, a protocol created in the wake of September 11 that was now being tested for the first time.

By that point, Democrats were experiencing more than a little buyer's remorse for their role in sending the House into uncharted territory and were antsy for a way out.

"Let's elect McHenry. This is no good," Jeffries's top aide, Gideon Bragin, texted me on October 24, adding that the overwhelming majority of his caucus was prepared to vote to empower McHenry as a caretaker Speaker.

Yet after a tense and unruly meeting of the House Republican conference, McHenry ultimately decided against putting himself forward for any such role—caretaker or otherwise—leaving everyone scratching their heads as to how the House would get out of this cul-de-sac.

* * *

Near the beginning of the multi-week search for a new Speaker, Kevin asked me to jot down a few bullets for a handwritten note that he wanted to leave his successor—similar to the letter left in the Oval Office from one president to the next.

So I drafted a letter for Steve Scalise. And then one for Jim Jordan. Then Tom Emmer. And finally, Patrick McHenry.

Exasperated and more than a little annoyed after ripping each of those four drafts up, I asked Kevin if he wanted me to continue with the exercise.

"Let's just address it: 'To Whom It May Concern,'" he joked.

The final recipient of that letter would end up being Mike Johnson of Louisiana, a little-known lawmaker at the time who was chosen at the conclusion of a late-night session by a beleaguered and bleary-eyed Republican conference entering their third week without anyone in charge.

The press dubbed him the "Accidental Speaker," but in my experience, very little in Washington was truly an accident. As you might recall, Johnson's name was written in during the initial conference balloting back in the fall, around the same time he had been approached by Virginia Representative Bob Good to run for the job. Likewise, Johnson's name was one of those floated by Andy Biggs as a member "who nobody's mad at ever"—which ultimately ended up being one of the main selling points for his candidacy.

Though Johnson has since publicly downplayed having any prior designs on the speakership, I harbor my doubts. If you look at the cover of this book or rewatch the voting from January, you'll see Kevin seated to my right and then the same member seated to my left each day without fail: Mike Johnson.

You know when you have a feeling that someone is peeking over your shoulder? That was how I felt with Mike the entire week, catching him more than once trying to eavesdrop on my conversations with Kevin or sneak a glimpse at some of my incoming text messages.

In fairness, Mike Johnson was far from the only one envisioning himself taking the gavel. Altogether, thirteen different individuals put their name forward to replace Kevin, in addition to two former members who even returned to the Capitol to test their viability. But it was Mike who found his way into the Speaker's chair—in a very different and more direct route than we carefully navigated over the previous ten-plus years.

Given the history you now know of House Republicans, avoiding the job and appearing that you don't want it has actually been a fairly successful strategy for getting it. If that was indeed the play, it worked—and proved once again that timing is everything in politics.

Dear Mike,

From one firefighter's son to another, congratulations on your election as Speaker of the House.

Make this role what you want it to be. Never do something just because "that's how it's been done before."

Pick some battles of your choosing—not simply the ones thrust upon you. Lasting change is possible with clear purpose and cheerful persistence.

Finally, open the House floor as often as you can. Each sunrise brings new opportunities—and breakthroughs are always closer than they seem.

My team and I stand ready to assist. Godspeed. Do great things.

Kevin

* * *

It just so happened that the day Mike Johnson was elected Speaker was a date that I had circled on my personal calendar for months.

After my brother was ordained a Catholic priest, Kevin's gift to him was an invitation to deliver the opening prayer for the House—which we scheduled a few months in advance for October 25.

As mentioned, I told Kevin about the fifteen prayers to St. Rita foreshadowing our fifteen ballots. While he shared the story with various audiences he addressed in the months that followed, he would also privately joke with me that maybe fifteen prayers was a bit excessive.

"Next time, tell your brother to send just one prayer!" Kevin chided.

Perhaps we should have been more specific, though, because immediately following my brother's prayer on October 25, the House elected its 56th Speaker, Mike Johnson.

Kevin took the podium to formally introduce Father Jeremy Leganski at noon, the last time he would ever be atop the Speaker's rostrum. Meanwhile, I bowed my head and wept as my brother led the House in prayer, with my dad and in-laws watching from the gallery above and Giulia draping her arm around me for support.

Good and gracious God: we praise you, we love you, and we thank you for this day.

Draw near to these Members of Congress. Remind them of their calling to serve the true common good. Help them to be instruments of unity, peace, and reconciliation—in our country and throughout the world.

Bless them, guide them, and fill them with an abundance of your grace. May they decide everything for the well-being of all and may they never turn aside from your will.

May all that they do begin from you, and by you, be brought to completion.

In your name, we pray, Amen.

That, too, would be the last day I would ever walk the House floor.

* * *

Just days after the fateful vote to remove Kevin, Israel was the target of a series of brutal and barbaric terrorist attacks carried out by Hamas that came to be known as the October 7 massacre. Unfortunately, because a permanent Speaker had not yet been elected, the House was unable to conduct any legislative business, including votes to provide critical aid to our closest ally in the Middle East.

When Mike Johnson was eventually elevated, he was perhaps overly sensitive to the far-right flank while finding his footing in the new role. Instead of sending a clean Israel aid bill to the President's desk and making law within his first week on the job, the new Speaker attempted to offset the cost of the Israel aid package by cutting from one of President Biden's signature legislative achievements, the so-called Inflation Reduction Act, thereby causing the bill to stall in the Democratic-run Senate.

What ensued was a monthslong standoff that held up not only aid to Israel, but also aid to Ukraine to assist in its efforts to fend off Vladimir Putin's ongoing military invasion. Who's to say how the world would have looked if those aid packages were passed in a more timely manner—though I imagine both nations might have some views on whether or not the six-month delay harmed their respective causes.

To help break the logjam, House Democrats began signaling in public and private that they would be willing to lend a hand to defeat any Motion to Vacate that might arise, provided that Johnson first bring a clean Ukraine aid bill to the floor.

"It does seem to me, based on informal conversations, that were Speaker Johnson to do the right thing relative to meeting the significant national security needs of the American people by putting it on the floor for an up-or-down vote," Minority Leader Hakeem Jeffries told *The New York Times*, "there will be a reasonable number of people in the House Democratic Caucus who will take the position that he should not fall as a result."

Personally, I have to imagine Democrats also felt more than a little responsible for the chaos that was unleashed after removing Kevin and were hesitant to send the House down that road again.

"Our job is really to govern and to make sure that we're having government be able to address the needs of the American people and not be non-functioning," Connecticut Democrat Rosa DeLauro remarked in defending her caucus' decision to support Johnson.

In the end, Speaker Johnson relented and allowed a clean vote on aid to Ukraine and Israel—a move that triggered a fresh Motion to Vacate against him from a group of eleven House Republicans. But this time around, Democrats came to the new Speaker's rescue, joining a bipartisan coalition that voted 359–43 to keep him in the Speaker's chair, bringing the high drama of the 118th Congress to a close.

CHAPTER 22

ONE FINAL THOUGHT

In reflecting upon the events of the past few years, my overarching takeaway is that we played the hand we were dealt as best we could, a brutal hand after the 2022 midterms produced such tight margins.

When it came to negotiating with the Freedom Caucus in the lead-up to January, Kevin was damned if he did or damned if he didn't—so he opted to move forward and do it.

Though our unique governing structure was not always pretty, it was producing results and has continued to prove effective even after our departure, with the Five Families still being called upon to hash out disagreements.

We passed the strongest border security bill in history, H.R. 2, a task that flummoxed larger Republican majorities of yesteryear given the thorny politics around immigration.

We brought about an end to the federal emergency declaration for the COVID-19 pandemic, while forcing President Biden to repeal several weak-on-crime initiatives enacted by the District of Columbia.

We showed that Republicans can fight and win on the issue of addressing our debt, with many of the same elements of Limit, Save, Grow and the Fiscal Responsibility Act forming the basis for the reforms included in the sweeping reconciliation bill enacted at the start of Trump's second term.

This on top of advancing other key Republican priorities, from energy production and educational freedom to supporting law enforcement and holding the Biden administration accountable.

Speaker Gingrich marveled at our ability to manage the unruly conference, remarking on more than one occasion that Kevin was a greater legislative tactician than he, himself, was as Speaker.

Less than a month before the Ethics Committee restarted its investigation into him, Matt Gaetz told CNN that he would give Kevin "an 'A'" for his performance as Speaker.

"I don't give it lightly," Gaetz said at the time. "I think he's done a good job."

Even Chip Roy begrudgingly credited Kevin for working with a "large number" of members "across the spectrum," saying that his method "largely worked." Perhaps that is why an AP poll taken in the wake of Kevin's removal vote found only one-quarter of Republicans approved of the decision.

* * *

One could argue that we should have applied more vinegar than honey, and I will admit that the Freedom Caucus' insistence throughout our negotiations that "no retribution" be levied against their members has popped into my head once or twice as a tantalizing "what if?"

It's not that we didn't consider it. In fact, near the end, we toyed with amending our conference rules to state that any member who introduced or supported a Motion to Vacate without concurrence of the conference would cease to be a member of the Republican conference. That could have resulted in Matt Gaetz and his cohorts automatically losing their committee assignments—a punishment that would have stung back home in their districts and perhaps made them think twice about moving forward.

Even so, I have my reasons to doubt that a hammer of this sort would have been a durable, long-term solution when it came to running the House. As Speaker Boehner once remarked, the job is to "keep 218 frogs in a wheelbarrow long enough to pass a bill"—and that would have become borderline impossible if we permanently jettisoned a handful of members from our ranks.

We even brought in professional help at one point, enlisting author and motivational speaker Pat Lencioni to speak at our party retreat in a quasi-therapist role. He hosted a multi-hour session to try to teach our adult members the skills necessary to work through their issues and build trust with one another. If the congressional budget were to allow for a full-time group therapist, it certainly couldn't hurt.

Despite the near-constant chaos, however, Kevin managed to excel in one of the toughest jobs in Washington in ways both big and small. From establishing the landmark bipartisan Select Committee on China, hosting Taiwanese President Tsai Ing-wen on American soil, and reforming the House Intelligence Committee, to befriending longtime institutional staff as he opened the House each day and carving out time to spontaneously meet visitors to the Capitol, there was no denying that this was a man uniquely qualified for the job at hand after years of trial by fire—which only made the way things ended all the more difficult to stomach.

* * *

Over the years, Kevin often finished his remarks to the conference with what he dubbed "One Final Thought"—a concluding quote, video, or story to punctuate the point he was trying to make that given week.

It was an effective technique—much like how a coach might motivate their team before a big game—and I always looked forward to helping him unearth the perfect final thought for whatever the moment required.

In that spirit, let me offer one final thought of both good news and bad news.

First, the bad news: The House Republican conference is structurally unstable, owing in large part to a Freedom Caucus that misunderstands the concept of legislative leverage they so often preach about. As a result, the House of Representatives is set to become only more ungovernable in the years to come absent changes to either the institution or the attitudes of the members who serve there.

During our fight, most conservatives claimed they wanted to "change Washington"—and I believe some of them were deeply earnest in that belief. Unfortunately, it is hard to see how this entire episode was anything more than a Pyrrhic victory for their cause. Instead, they have remained mostly allergic to doing the things needed to actually change Washington, especially during instances of divided government: namely, taking half a loaf when you can get it, winning elections, then coming back for more.

Put differently, you can't expect to change much when your only vote is no. And trust me, our counterparts on the Democratic side of the aisle knew this and counted upon us not being able to put up 218 Republican votes on our own—leaving us to essentially fight with one arm tied behind our back whenever we were forced to enter into legislative negotiations with them.

Think about it for a moment: Hard right conservatives got their preferred man in the Speaker's chair in Mike Johnson and *still* were unhappy. Moreover, it is not clear that federal policy moved to the right in any meaningful way during the 118th Congress after swapping out Kevin.

"Switching from McCarthy to Johnson was the biggest mistake I've seen conservatives make in my decade of serving in Congress," Kentucky Representative Thomas Massie later remarked.

Even Tucker Carlson added, "I think those of us who thought kicking Kevin McCarthy out of leadership [was a good idea]…we were completely wrong and I think it's important to admit that."

If anything, the outcomes became more liberal for the remainder of the 118th Congress, with government spending going up, multiple additional continuing resolutions passed, and marquee Republican priorities left on the cutting-room floor.[*] Meanwhile, our national debt rocketed past $36 trillion—with an additional trillion dollars being added to the red every hundred days—and neither party has moved any closer to having an honest discussion about the entitlement system that is overwhelmingly responsible for putting us on a path to fiscal insolvency.

For all their reverence for our Constitution, I am curious how many of our Freedom Caucus friends could recall that our nation's founding document was, itself, the by-product of a compromise: a grand bargain between the large states and small states that resulted in coequal branches of government continually engaged in a tug-of-war for both policy and public opinion.

---

[*]	House Republicans also went on to lose seats in the 2024 elections—all while President Trump reclaimed the White House and Senate Republicans added to their ranks that same year.

Unfortunately, if this small yet determinative bloc of Freedom Caucus members continues to insist on their all-or-nothing mentality, the left will continue to take half steps further and further in their direction while Republicans cede the playing field entirely, draped in a jersey of purity.

Part of this dynamic is structural: The current House district maps essentially provide both parties with a floor of two hundred seats, give or take—leaving fewer than thirty true swing seats that determine control of the chamber. That number is on track to sink even lower after the wave of 2026 midcycle redistricting. As a result, the only real election for the vast majority of lawmakers becomes their primary, which in turn encourages members to cater more and more to the bases of their respective parties.

In addition, the Freedom Caucus has essentially become a quixotic third party that simply chooses to caucus with Republicans when convenient— meaning that even when Republicans have a majority on paper, the fragile coalition is subject to dissolution depending on the day of the week. This helps explain why once-routine votes to keep the government open have become drawn out life-or-death grudge matches, consuming much of congressional Republican leaders' time at the expense of tackling other pressing issues facing Americans.

*　*　*

Speaking of such issues, I have often reflected upon the story of Democratic representative Marcy Kaptur of Ohio, the gentlewoman you might recall briefly considered crossing party lines to vote for Kevin for Speaker during the fourteenth ballot.

In 1987, Kaptur introduced legislation to construct a national memorial in Washington, DC for US World War II veterans. She reintroduced her bill in subsequent Congresses in 1989 and 1991, finally seeing it enacted into law in 1993.

In other words, it took one representative six years to secure legislation for arguably one of the most sympathetic public causes you could possibly imagine in our nation—that of honoring the greatest generation, who fought and died for the cause of freedom.

Unfortunately, I fear that fewer and fewer current members would be willing to put in that sort of time and effort for the causes they supposedly hold dear—many of which would undoubtedly take more effort, skill, and persistence to see to completion. Rather, I foresee a rise in the one-off political sugar-high votes—measures to censure, expel, impeach, vacate, subpoena, hold in contempt of Congress, or any other similar votes that are designed to excite the party base and juice fundraising, but do little in the way of achieving anything meaningful for the American people.

As former Speaker Sam Rayburn of Texas once remarked: "Any jackass can kick down a barn, but it takes a good carpenter to build one."

Regrettably, we now have a political system where scalps sell, division is profit, and our incentive structure—from the proliferation of social media to the imperative of appeasing the base and maximizing small-dollar donations—rewards the behavior of jackasses over that of carpenters.

* * *

Of course, this turmoil and upheaval is not limited to the Republican side of the aisle. Most notably, we witnessed an extraordinary occurrence when President Joe Biden was forced out of running for reelection by members of his own party in July 2024, just weeks before the Democratic National Convention.

You better believe that as Washington and America debated whether or not Biden would drop out in the wake of his disastrous debate performance, I was running a mental check of how closely the sitting president was following our strategy from January 2023 for fending off an internal rebellion.

Rule #1: Always Have the Candidate Be Visible

Nope—Biden disappeared for over a week after the debate. When he did reemerge in interviews or unscripted events, the results were decidedly mixed, and the gaffes continued.

Rule #2: Be More Organized Than the Opposition

Once again, Biden failed on this front—only calling small pockets of lawmakers belatedly and allowing the chorus of naysayers to quickly snowball to a point where his candidacy became untenable.

Rule #3: Never Let an Alternate Pick Up Steam

Strike three. Vice President Kamala Harris and her allies played this scenario masterfully, fully backing the incumbent president in public, while coalescing support behind the scenes and making the case that passing over a woman of color would wreak incalculable havoc inside the fragile Democratic coalition.

Not surprisingly, when Biden made the historic announcement that he would forgo seeking reelection, it was Vice President Harris who was quickly anointed.

Having surveyed this landscape, I told anyone who asked that it was only a matter of *when*, not if, President Biden would depart the race—in spite of his and his team's consistent calls that they were staying in for the long haul. Moreover, this episode served as further proof to me that there was nothing magical about a Motion to Vacate button. If a determined group wants to grind things to a halt and force an individual out, there are many ways they can do so.

* * *

So . . . where do we go from here?

For one, although Kevin might have needed to become the sacrificial lamb for the cause, it would be encouraging if a bipartisan majority of the House were more willing to step in and tamp down frivolous motions to vacate the Speaker, as they were when it came to Speaker Johnson in 2024. Holding any leader to the standard that they must have 100 percent support from their party at all times is only a recipe for inaction and paralysis.

This could also be achieved with enough members from both sides linking arms to amend the opening-day rules package to remove the single-member Motion to Vacate, which we have now seen cannot be trusted in the hands of members like Matt Gaetz.

Alternatively, House Republicans could take a page from the Senate and treat the speakership as they treat the position of Senate president pro tempore: electing the longest-tenured member of the conference to serve in a largely ceremonial role at the top, while vesting the lion's share of the power, staff, and budget with the party's majority leader. In fact, such a nonpartisan Speaker model is the norm in many parliaments around the world, from the United Kingdom to Australia.

This change would enable the Republican leader to be accountable to a simple majority of the conference rather than the more unattainable and undesirable standard of near-unanimity, in turn allowing them greater latitude to make the decisions they think are best without fearing for their job every day. It would also serve as a fitting end to the Curse of the Majority Leader.

Finally, we can do more to send good people to Washington, while retiring those who are only in it for themselves.

In a welcome development, Freedom Caucus Chair Bob Good of Virginia—one of the eight who voted to remove Kevin—was defeated in his primary election in July 2024.

Including Good, six of Gaetz's eight useful idiots will no longer be in Congress come 2027—whether through resignation, retirement, defeat, or pursuit of a different political office.

Turns out there's not much for the Jokers to do when Batman is gone.

Speaking of our archenemy, Matt Gaetz was briefly considered for the position of Attorney General at the start of President Trump's second term, only to drop out a week later in no small part due to renewed scrutiny over his alleged unseemly behavior as a member, as well as lingering resentment from US senators for his actions toward Kevin.

Gaetz went so far as to abruptly resign from Congress in an apparent attempt to halt the House Ethics Committee investigation into his conduct. In the end, the bipartisan panel found substantial evidence that the disgraced former Florida congressman paid tens of thousands of dollars to women for sex or drugs on at least twenty occasions, including paying a seventeen-year-old girl for sex in 2017.

Though Gaetz has denied the findings, the truth always has a way of coming to light, and I have faith that America is beginning to grow wise to the ruse that some of these members are pulling. Maybe there is some justice in the world after all.

Even so, in the months that followed Kevin's removal, a wave of retirements struck House Republicans, many of whom cited exasperation at the ongoing dysfunction in the House as one of their main reasons for departing. This included members like Cathy McMorris Rodgers of Washington and Mike Gallagher of Wisconsin, both sitting chairs of powerful committees who chose to leave the House rather than complete their terms in their leadership.

"We've turned Congress into a 'greenroom' for Fox News and MSNBC, instead of being the key institution of government," Gallagher lamented upon his exit.

Closer to home, Patrick McHenry announced that he would not be seeking reelection in 2024, as did Garret Graves, who was redistricted into an unwinnable seat in his home state of Louisiana. Garret's misfortune particularly stung after he chose to pass on a run for governor early in 2023 in favor of helping Kevin run the House.

That is not to say there are not great people serving, members and staff alike. In my experience, the good far outnumber the bad, most of whom are doing the right things for the right reasons far from the headlines that dominate cable news. I hope I was able to highlight at least a few of those individuals in the pages of this book. But the good ones desperately need reinforcements and a system—as well as an electorate—that values workhorses rather than show horses.

As for me, Giulia and I moved to the suburbs and welcomed our first child in July 2024, a beautiful baby girl. Giulia still works on the Hill, and I happily root on her work as a chief counsel for the Energy and Commerce committee—including legislation that she and her team spearheaded to force a divestment of the popular social media app TikTok from its ties to the Chinese Communist Party.

Despite all that occurred, in talking to so many members of Team McCarthy in the months that followed, I don't think there is a single one of us who would not go back and do it all over again in a heartbeat if given the chance. That should tell you something. We received a master class in politics, negotiation, communication, psychology, leadership, and crisis management learning up close with Kevin, making friends and memories in the process that will last us a lifetime. More importantly, we made a real difference in people's lives through our work. I feel truly fortunate to have been a part of such an incredible team, and I will always be proud of what we accomplished together.

Therein lies the good news and a more positive final thought to those who care about our nation, especially our young people: Get involved. The most important word in our Constitution is its very first—"We"—an enduring invitation to serve. This experiment we call America depends upon our active civic engagement, and the quality of the decisions our government makes is directly tied to the quality of individuals making them. So volunteer, study the issues, vote, apply for an internship, join a campaign, even consider running for local or state office someday.

Take it from me: You never know where it might lead you.

ACKNOWLEDGMENTS

"Observation unrecorded is knowledge lost."

—James Ronda

This book was made possible through the love and support of many family members, friends, and colleagues over the years who encouraged me to write down my experiences and share them with the world.

Of course, this story starts with my family, especially my parents, Gerard and Julie Leganski, and my siblings, Jeremy and Sarah.

To Mom and Dad: Thank you for instilling in us our core values of faith, family, hard work, and a love of learning. I do not think I truly realized until becoming a parent how much you both did and how much you both sacrificed so that your children could pursue their callings. This book is a testament to those many sacrifices—big and small—and I can only hope to live up to your example as I raise my own family.

To Jeremy and Sarah: Thank you for always pushing me to be my best, while never hesitating to keep me humble. "Never give up" was a longstanding rule in the Leganski household that we all lived by, and I'm convinced our shared competitive streak was born in the backyard in Darien. Though the first job I ever had was being your big brother, I look up to you both in more ways than you know.

To my loving wife, Giulia, my everything. For all the ups and downs that DC presented, I am forever grateful that it led me to you. You are my rock and my best friend, you are an absolutely incredible mother, and I am so excited for the future we are building together. I love you.

To the Giannangeli family—especially Al, Cecile, Michael, and Vivian—thank you for welcoming me with open arms from the start and providing me a home away from home in Washington. No matter how bad a week might have been, it was always comforting to know there was a warm bowl of pasta and a nice bottle of red waiting at the end of the tunnel.

At its core, this book is fundamentally about the power of the speakership, and I greatly benefited from the support of not one, but two former Speakers in this endeavor.

First, thank you to Speaker McCarthy for graciously sharing your personal notes, stories, and recollections of a two-decade-plus life in politics—including several interviews specifically for this project. Each time we spoke, I gleaned a new anecdote or insight and was reminded of just how sharp your decision-making skills are in the arena. The House is certainly worse off without your determined leadership and unyielding optimism, and you will always be #1 in my book.

Thank you also to Speaker Gingrich, a veritable fountain of knowledge across so many subjects—and perhaps the quickest responder to emails I have ever encountered. I greatly benefited from your experience of publishing multiple bestselling books, and I also have you to thank for personally connecting me with the agent who made this book possible.

Speaking of, I am deeply grateful to my fearless agent, Kathy Lubbers, who took a flyer on me and this project without ever having met me. As a first-time author, I probably required more hand-holding than most, but your dogged persistence helped carry this through to the end.

My sincere thanks to Tony Lyons of Skyhorse who recognized the potential in this story from the start and gave it a home. Many thanks to Jason Katzman and his team, as well, for their careful edits, steady guidance, and help sharpening the narrative along the way. It was a true pleasure to work with you to bring this vision to life.

Thank you to all the members of Team McCarthy, from beginning to end. In particular, I would like to acknowledge the members of our senior staff in the Speaker's Office: Dan Meyer, James Min, Machalagh Carr, Alexandra Gourdikian DiCicco, Natalie Joyce, Matt Sparks, Brittan Specht, Mark Bednar, Tim Monahan, Caleb Smith, and Kim Hamm, as well as Kyle

Lombardi in the personal office. Politics is a team sport, and I could not have asked for a better crew to be in the trenches with, day in and day out.

I was especially fortunate to be blessed with such a loyal floor team: Chris Bien, Cullen Murphy, Jordan Dayer, Charlie Homan, and Ella Gunn. You worked the long hours and dealt with members at their best and worst, but I always knew the House floor was in good hands with our team. On a personal note, watching each of your careers blossom from the outside has been one of the most rewarding experiences of my time off the Hill. Do great things.

Special thanks here goes to Cullen Murphy, the first person I entrusted to read the first draft of my then extremely half-baked manuscript. You read it in its entirety on a flight to Florida and said, "John, we have something here." Your unwavering faith in this project from the start kept me going at multiple impasses where I was ready to throw in the towel. Simply put, this book would not have happened without your constant encouragement and assistance, which spanned everything from research and fact-checking to copyediting and marketing. Everyone needs someone in their corner repeating "Yes, you can" when you're convinced that you cannot—and you were that person for me in this effort. Thank you, brother.

Thank you also to James Min, whose feedback on early drafts and final copyediting was invaluable. More importantly, thank you for plucking my internship application out of the pile and changing the course of my life. Everyone on Team McCarthy owes you a debt of gratitude for your mentorship and generosity, and I sincerely appreciate all of the opportunities you afforded me throughout my career. When I first came to DC as a young staffer, my dad asked you to "take care of my son"—and you certainly held up your end of the bargain.

Finally, to all of the institutional staff of the House of Representatives: the parliamentarians, clerks, Sergeant at Arms, chamber security, Capitol Police, protective detail, and everyone in between. It was a pleasure getting to know and learn from so many of you over the years, and I still treasure our late-night chats and early-morning hellos.

Special recognition here goes to House Parliamentarians Tom Wickham and Jason Smith, Miss Pat and Miss Doris in the cloakroom, Joyce Hamlett,

Wallace Simpson, Chris Fischer, Darius Holmes, Jesse Foster, Keith Pernie, Chris Stoehr, Isaac Yowell, and countless others.

You are the true civil servants who keep the institution running, and you deserve far more thanks than you will ever receive. Regardless of who sits atop the Speaker's rostrum, the first branch of government will continue moving forward because of dedicated people like you working diligently behind the scenes.

God bless.

ABOUT THE AUTHOR

John Leganski is a political strategist and former senior congressional adviser who served as Deputy Chief of Staff to House Speaker Kevin McCarthy.

One of the most visible aides on Capitol Hill following his role as McCarthy's top-floor lieutenant during the historic contest for Speaker, Leganski was the youngest floor directory in House history and held senior roles in every major House leadership office—including the Majority Whip, Majority Leader, Minority Leader, and Speaker.

Credited with devising the internal strategy that jump-started House passage of the landmark Tax Cuts and Jobs Act, Leganski was at the center of every major policy debate in Washington during the first Trump and Biden administrations—from the federal pandemic response to negotiating the Fiscal Responsibility Act to raise the debt ceiling. He also helped author the Commitment to America agenda that anchored Republicans' successful campaign to win back the House in 2022.

His work has been cited by national publications and media outlets, including CNN, *Politico*, *Roll Call*, *The Hill*, *Punchbowl News*, and *The Washington Examiner*, while his post-Congress insights have been published by *The Wall Street Journal* and are regularly read by Fortune 100 companies, start-ups, trade associations, and coalitions inside and outside the beltway.

He now serves as a partner at Harbinger Strategies, a leading government and political affairs firm, where he advises clients across the private sector on legislative strategy, policy development, and political risk.

A native of suburban Chicago, Leganski is a graduate of Stanford University and a former writer for *The Stanford Review*. He currently resides in Potomac, Maryland, with his wife and their children.